How To Suck Less At Estimating

Habits for Better Project Outcomes

By Jonathan L. Isaacson,
The Intentional Restorer

Printed in the United States of America
First Printing, June 2022
ISBN: 978-1-7356227-7-4

Published by The DYOJO
thedyojo.com

Library of Congress Control Number: 2022912003

Early Testimonials For This Book

Jon provides incredible insight, systems, processes, and accountability for running the estimating and administrative side of our business that is severely lacking in knowledge and expertise. A must-read for current or aspiring estimators. - **Chad Brandt, WLS, Owner of PuroClean of Chandler (AZ)**

The content is detailed enough to be highly useful and informative, yet still simple enough that they're easily understood and followed by a novice. This is yet another great resource of many more to come. **- Randy Carley, National Response Supervisor (WA)**

Another unbelievable addition to the *Be Intentional* series from Mr. Isaacson. It's so refreshing to finally see all of this often-guarded information transcribed from an industry expert to words on a page. This book will surely help anyone who reads it! **- Josh Zolin, CEO of Windy City Equipment, Author of *Blue is the New White* (AZ)**

The way Jon Isaacson points out the simple truths about estimating is refreshing and makes him a genius. I just think it's a stupid book because I wish I had written it! Watch out world, the Intentional Restorer has just flipped the tables on how information is presented in the insurance/restoration industry...transparency is king. *- Chris Stanley Founder of IA Path & Author of the Insurance Adjuster Playbook Series 8x Amazon Best Seller* (FL)

I have found Jon's books and his podcast to be the most informative for our industry. His content reinforces the beliefs I had in my 15 years in this industry. His podcasts can be listened to during the massive amount of windshield time we all have in this industry. I mention the Be Intentional series of books regularly when speaking with our franchises on being the best restorers we can be, both at the franchise and the franchisor level. **- Keith Nelson, Senior Commercial Project Consultant at Paul Davis USA (NC)**

As usual, Jon provides great material with actionable details. This book hits a lot of key points that are part of the estimating game that estimators need to understand in order to be successful. Sometimes we get so busy turning out estimates that we miss the chance to learn from other points of view that can make us better estimators; this book is one of those resources. **- David Smith, *still* recovering from insurance work (OR)**

The connection that Jon has with the content he writes about is next level. If you've ever met Jon, you can envision these meaningful words coming out of his mouth. This book is yet another demonstration of his love for our industry **- Josh Winton, IAQ Josh, Owner at Discrete Air Quality (FL)**

Jon hits the nail on the head again. His insight into the industry can help all restorers easily understand the process and procedures to help them succeed. I can't wait for book #5. **- Rob MacPherson, Manager of National Estimating Services at DKI Canada**

Jon should write a new book and just have 10,000 pages where only this sentence appears once in the middle of every page, "The quality of the data inputs (composed estimate) is in direct correlation to the quality of the data captured." Jon once again knocks it out of the park. **- Mathew Allen, Founder and Executive Producer at AdjusterTV (MT)**

Mostly, I felt seen, I felt heard. I couldn't wait to read not only the next chapter but the entire book. It is clear that there are steps I need to take in order to change things. I don't know all of them yet, but I can't wait for the book to come out so that I can shorten my DANG learning curve! **- Thea Tapson, Restoration Project Coordinator (NV)**

What I love about this book is it serves, in many ways, as a textbook that combines theory with Jon's fun writing style and practical application of the concepts within the book. If you have estimators, I highly suggest making this required reading for your estimating crew. **- Eric Sprague, Co-Founder of Super Tech University (UT)**

This book is a must-read for any property restoration professional. Jon leverages his own vast experience, as well as the wisdom of industry experts, to deliver a value-focused guide to the world of estimating. Everything you need to know, to take your skills to the next level, is between these two covers. **- Josh Diaz, Industry Sales Rep (TN)**

This book is well-written and insightful. Learning to scope and write an estimate is one thing. But Jon also shared his knowledge and experience of interacting with adjusters. This is invaluable. **- Peter J. Crosa, Independent Adjuster, Business Owner, and author of *Soft Selling Hardened Claims Adjusters* (FL)**

Jon is an industry veteran that has always strived to push the industry in a positive direction. He puts forth a lot of time and

effort into bringing the industry together through training and discussions on different topics. As someone who has been in this industry for over a decade, I appreciate what Jon is doing to continue into the future. **- Mitch Heitman, Regional Director of Operations, FIRST ONSITE (IL)**

Having read all 3 of Jon's books, and listening to many of his podcasts, I can say I'm a better estimator/manager because of it. His content is a must-read (and listen-to) if you want to be a player in this game. **- John Slater, Owner at Celtic Mold Assessments (NY)**

"With his latest book, Jon Isaacson again demonstrates why he is a "go to" resource for so many people in the property restoration industry. He has the genuine heart of a teacher, and it comes through in every chapter of How To Not Suck At Estimating." **- Luke Draeger, Author (WA)**

Table of Contents

Foreword

By Lisa Lavender

Nothing else matters if you suck at estimating. You can have the best service, and be the most effective at delivering quality restoration services, but if you <u>suck</u> at estimating it may be all for nothing. After over 20 years in the industry as an operator and trainer, I have reviewed many estimates, observing and documenting the best and worst practices. After reading his first book, *Be Intentional: Estimating*, I thought, "YES! Jon Isaacson nailed it!"

This book is not just for new and seasoned estimators, it is for anyone who operates or manages a restoration company of any size. Jon lays out the principles of effective estimating. If you practice what he preaches, you will build a foundation to create clearly defined expectations and best practices in your estimating process. Elevating your estimating habits will generate clearer road maps for your team to deliver consistently more excellent project outcomes.

Sucking at estimating in the construction industry is a leadership issue. It is the result of applying the <u>worst</u> practices for an essential function that regularly result in the <u>worst</u> outcomes. Poor estimating habits will impact job profitability, company credibility, and your company's ability to build long-term relationships in the local market.

The **estimate** in the restoration industry is unique. Although we use the term estimate, this document often serves multiple functions such as the bid, the contract, and the invoice.

- It represents the scope of work and the cost (budget) for the execution of a project.
- It also serves the purpose of telling the story of what and why your team did what they did on a project.
- It outlines the billing details that can expedite or delay payment for services rendered.

When estimating is approached and executed with the right mindset and values, it serves as the foundation for building long term relationships based on trust with customers and carriers. An accurate estimate allows you to work towards establishing clearly agreed-upon scopes and prices. A structured and detailed bid facilitates both a positive impression as well as the means to address any questions in a constructive manner. A thoroughly written estimate tells the story of your company's approach to serving the client. Profitability, or lack thereof, starts with your estimating process.

You have a lot riding on your estimating practices. In this new book and the accompanying course, Jon breaks down the mindsets and habits that serve as the keys to success. Of course, he does so in his signature entertaining style (INFOtainment), which makes the educational content easy to digest and apply. His unique approach is what inspired me to ask him to develop a course based on the principles from his first book. I am thrilled to release this course through Restoration Technical Institute as I know it will be equal parts practical and entertaining for everyone who attends.

As you embark with *The Intentional Restorer* on the next leg of his journey, this book and course will give you the tools to employ THE DYOJO Way for your success to:

Do it right
Do it efficiently
Do it excellently

Preface

This book is a companion to a course, by the same title, the DYOJO created in collaboration with our friends at Restoration Technical Institute (RTI).

This book is stands alone. You can and will learn something by reading it cover to cover or referring to it as needed.

This book is a companion. Shortening your DANG learning curve will be enhanced by the videos shared with participants in the course.

As an owner or manager, you may be reading this book looking for something to supplement the training efforts in your organization. In this era where we are fighting labor shortages and tempted to buy into the negative perceptions of the incoming workforce, Anthony Nelson, President of Premier Restoration, shares some valuable insights. He says, "Quite often our younger Millennial and Gen Z technicians will refuse to tackle a given task until they understand the 'why.'" New managers and even many seasoned owners alike are tempted to reply, "Because I told you so," but find this mindset doesn't net the result they are seeking. Nelson shares how he had to learn to change his habits,

> *"This was annoying to me at first because all I wanted to do was train as I was trained. It seemed easier to simply bark orders than it did to spend additional time explaining the 'why.' Years later, I can tell you this was very short-sighted. Explaining the 'why' behind each of these steps to odor mitigation meant I didn't have to repeat myself. The knowledge just stuck[1]."*

This book, and the accompanying course, are NOT designed to be how-to's for estimating. Our focus will be insurance claims and the primary tool we will discuss is an estimating software called Xactimate. Yet, I believe many of these principles are helpful to the broader context of estimating in the skilled trades as well as

---

[1] Nelson, A (2022, February 18) *Incorporating The "Why" Into Odor Removal Training*. C & R Magazine. https://candrmagazine.com/incorporating-the-why-into-odor-removal-training

for those restoration companies who have chosen not to use the aforementioned program.

Better Project Outcomes

This book, and the accompanying course, are designed to be helpful in developing the right mindset and habits for achieving better project outcomes by addressing the first factor in the project lifecycle, the estimate. **Do you want better or more consistent project outcomes?** Everything I share has been battle-tested. If I know anything that is of value, it is because it has been etched into my process by getting my teeth kicked in. Failure is the best teacher if you are willing to learn from it.

If you are looking for shortcuts, hacks, or ninja moves, you may find a few. The DYOJO stands for The **D**o **Y**our **O**wn **J**ob **D**ojo. When you train yourself in the mindset and habits for success, you will better lead yourself and others towards your shared goals. If your team is struggling to work together in harmony, it is likely a trust issue and the only way to correct that is for every team member to be accountable for doing their own job.

While too many want to pontificate on the meaning and building of trust, it is no simpler than what I just expressed. If I don't trust that you are doing your job, to the best of your abilities (this does not mean without mistakes) there will be no teamwork. On the other hand, if I can trust that you are doing your job, even if I don't fully like you, we can work together as a team because we trust each other to be about handling our business.

Why do I bring this up in a book about estimating habits? Well, my target audience is fourfold:

The **aspiring professional** who wants to advance in their career. This book will be helpful to you. But, if you are not committed to mastering your current role (DYOJO), you will struggle to climb any further than where you are now. You will see how the things you are doing now will prepare you for future responsibilities.

Estimators and project managers who want to level up their abilities in estimating, claims negotiations, and project outcomes. This book covers a lot of what I have discussed in articles and two of my prior three books (Book 1 and 3). There is a good deal of new content as well, including deeper dives into some technical aspects of estimating.

The **new manager** who has been thrown into a position without much training or direction. This book will be helpful to you in understanding some of the principles that go into creating clarity, consistency, and accountability for your team. All three of my prior books will be of use to you as you develop your leadership skills.

The **business owner** who either needs some direction or another voice sharing these core principles. This book will be helpful to you and every member of your team as you build an interdependent organization. I am sure you will want to buy multiple copies so that you can hand them out like candy to every employee.

I will try to pick away at some of those faulty foundations I believe regularly lead to profit-sucking estimating habits. In doing this I will try to break out those mindsets that are particularly helpful for the categories of professionals listed above. By the end of this book, and course, you should have <u>at least</u> **six elements that every estimator needs in their toolbag for success**. I hope you enjoy this book and I look forward to your honest feedback.

The author, Ed Cross, Lily Atkins, Gordy Powell, & Miranda K9
Lambert at RIA 2022 - Photo credit Sean Atkins

Module One

Dumb by Design vs. Dumb Design

You have made a commitment to read a book titled *How To Suck Less At Estimating*, so either you are willing to admit that you, or "someone you know", needs some assistance with <u>developing your estimating process</u>.

If you bought this book,
does it mean you suck at estimating?
No.

If someone bought this book for you,
does it mean you suck at estimating?
No.

Before we dive into the meat of this course, let's take a minute to discuss our choice of polemical selection of words. I enjoy when people are able to take a word or a concept that I commonly use and expose that I have been using it incorrectly. Whether it's a book, a podcast, or even a movie, those ah-ha moments have a way of sticking with me when I am slapped around by simple logic. To that end, one of the best books on personal development that I have ever read emerged from within our industry.

Rachel Stewart, then Executive VP of Titan Restoration and now CEO/Founder of Xcelerate Restoration Software, wrote *Unqualified Success*[2]. She flipped the idea of "sucking" on its head, when she said, "***The <u>only</u> qualification to get better: being willing to suck when you start.***"

We all start out being dumb, or sucking at something. Maybe you don't suck, but you would like to elevate your ability to consistently achieve better project outcomes. Join the club! If you

---

[2] Read more in my review of *Unqualified Success* in R&R Magazine - https://www.randrmagonline.com/articles/88591-are-you-ready-to-be-an-unqualified-success

are willing to admit you suck or that you feel dumb, you've come to the right place. <u>Being dumb when you start is normal. Staying dumb is a decision.</u> I'll do my best to share what I have learned over two decades in this industry, but understand - **you are not alone**. Better estimating outcomes are the result of intentional, if not dumbed-down or fool proof, processes.

When I am frustrated with a project it's often a result of me allowing busyness to drag me back into bad habits. Personal development challenges each of us to fight against the status quo. Participating in these cycles of mediocrity is rooted in the mindsets and practices we know don't work, yet we continue to fall back upon. .

In business, we throw around the concept that we want to "Mc-Donald-ize" our processes. In practice, this means that we remove as many user errors as possible. It means that we train with as much clarity and consistency as possible so that even a newcomer can be successful and held accountable for the process. *While you may be tempted to think that your team members are stupid, what likely is a more effective assessment is whether your process isn't dumb enough.*

My goal in *Be Intentional: Estimating* was to help aspiring professionals set themselves up for success. Many of our setbacks stem from our odd infatuation with over-complicating everything. Keeping it simple will go a long way to making progress in your process. If you were to tell me that my first book was <u>dumb</u>, I would take that as a high compliment.

My book being dumb is not a moral qualification, it is a by-product of its design. There are many processes that have been frustratingly dumbed down and <u>yet</u> if you take a step back to look more broadly at them you realize they have followed their blueprint. You may be thinking of many such systems within the insurance ecosystem, it is important for all of us as intentional restorers to distinguish between <u>dumb by design</u> and <u>dumb design</u>.

Have you ever heard of **a dumb terminal**? My friend Roger Howson, a public adjuster out of Seattle, introduced me to this term during an interview on The DYOJO Podcast about insurance appraisals[3]. He mentioned that many adjusters have become dumb terminals and explained that he did not mean this as a slight on their abilities but rather an observation of the modern process of claims adjusting.

> *"A dumb terminal is a terminal that does not perform local processing of entered information, but serves only as an input/output device for an attached or network-linked processor[4]."*

There are so many layers of compliance and review in the claims process that many adjusters have little autonomy or authority. You may think they are dumb but you often are dealing with a process that is **dumb by design**. As a contractor, using a pessimistic lens, this process creates complexity and delays in the system. If we step back and look at it through the lens of the insurer, they have created a network of checks and balances in the pursuit of claims consistency. If your process does not account for this reality it is a **dumb design**.

We are not going to spend a lot of time in this book diving into the historical reasons for the shift, things have transformed from,

> Autonomous insurance agents who used to be intimately involved in the claims process and even paid for some claims out of their local offices;

> Local adjusters would walk a damaged structure with the contractor and negotiate with authority.

The system is what it is now. We can argue about improving it, but it isn't likely that it will revert to "the good ol' days" that restorers with more than 15 years of experience yearn for. I believe it is more productive to discuss where we go from here,

> rather than continuously lament what has been lost. By design, dumb computer terminals were key factors in the process of

---

[3] Episode 74 - https://www.youtube.com/watch?v=vv6zu-UCH4Y

[4] https://www.gartner.com/en/information-technology/glossary/dumb-terminal

information sharing (relays) before the internet. The insurance claims process is an information-sharing enterprise, which we will dive further into in the next Module.

PC Magazine states that terminals were "dumb",

> *"Because they usually did not contain the capabilities of a general-purpose computer (however, many terminals of the 1980s did contain special-purpose software and were far smarter than the "dumb" name implies)[5]."*

Dumb meant that their overall purpose was to function as pass-through devices. In the process of creating, submitting, and reviewing insurance claims estimates, contractors are frustrated when an item is held up by one of the relays (terminals) in this sequence. It would be dumb to not observe the review process as a whole, rather than only through the lens of how it affects the individual contractor.

Before we point too many fingers at the "other side", the owners, managers, and estimators from "this side" need to assess whether there is a malfunction in their habits leading to less than satisfactory project outcomes. If insurance uses dumb terminals by design, how are restorers structuring their terminals for transmitting information, internally as well as externally, in the estimating process? *Could your process, and outcomes, benefit from a bit of dumbing down?*

Pop Quiz: Identifying Dumb Aspects of the Process

Your estimators complain that they don't have the documentation they need to write an accurate estimate (or invoice) for mitigation services.

The general manager gets mad, "We just talked about this last week (and the week before that)."

If we fill in the blanks, everyone talked about doing things differently, but if we are honest, the technicians have come to expect these bi-monthly meetings telling them how terrible they

---

[5] Edwards, B. (2016, October 13) *The Forgotten World of Dumb Terminals*. PC Magazine. https://www.pcmag.com/news/the-forgotten-world-of-dumb-terminals

are at their jobs and everyone seems to have accepted that this is how it's going to be. It's a dance with no rhythm.

The general manager sends out an angry email, "Tomorrow we are having an all-hands meeting". It doesn't matter what ANYone is doing, EVERYone is going to be there.

The team knows what comes next because they have all been there. Week after week, it's the same sad song. Managers and estimators pile on, "If you [technicians] don't get your act together and get us the documentation that we need, you <u>may</u> [we're all more careful with these demands in the current labor market] find yourself looking for employment elsewhere!"

Even if the managers and estimators took a nicer approach, using a calm tone and trying to relate to the team saying, "Hey buds, we could really use your help [once again] to get this documentation. If you could do that, it would be super appreciated. You're the best." The net result is the same, zero change at any level.

If this is you, are you willing to ask yourself whether you <u>actually</u> did anything to alter your habits?

- Have you dug beneath the surface to identify causes for these issues?
- Have you updated or upgraded how you educate your team?
- Have you cross-trained technicians with estimators?
- Have you added any resources that help field staff to better capture and share information?

Estimating is an integrated <u>process</u>. Every terminal (team member) plays a key role in the transfer of information. No relay is more important than the others, even if we think some of them are dumb (or stupid). Information from the worksite is gathered (thorough data capture).

- The data capture is transferred into data input (an estimate).

- Estimates go through an internal review process[6] to create consistency in scoping, negotiating, and producing (See Exhibit 5)
- The story of the loss is relayed to the customer and the carrier through the estimate and supporting documentation.
- Once the estimate becomes an agreed-upon scope, a contract is made and the details are downloaded to the production team in a manner that sets them up for success.

As the owner, manager, estimator, and aspiring restoration professional, you decide whether the data transfers as seamlessly as possible. You decide, through the design of your process, whether you will develop and improve habits leading to better project outcomes. Incomplete data transfer, lackluster estimates, and poor contract clarity will lead to ongoing issues with completing projects on time, on budget, and to your customers satisfaction.

Perhaps the current labor issues are casting another perspective on areas where contractors can learn from carriers. Maybe there is a place for owners and managers to dumb down their processes and rethink the design of their terminals.

A common example:

We have a skilled technician who intuitively knows the work that needs to be done but struggles with paperwork, are there creative ways that we can free that person up to do what they are most competent at, which is also what the organization most benefits from them doing, and pair them with a centralized coordinator who can assist with the documentation? Probably not; we should expect everyone to be excellent at everything[7].

---

[6] For some insights on developing your internal claims review process, read the article *Help, Claims Review Shredded My Estimate* - https://www.randrmagonline.com/articles/88728-help-claims-review-shredded-my-estimate-the-intentional-restorer-vol-2-with-video

[7] Sarcasm

So, what about you? As an estimator, you write estimates. For the majority of the skilled trades, that estimate is sent directly to the customer.

You will discuss the scope, cost, and duration of the project and come to an agreement with the customer. The customer will pay you directly for your goods and services. Documentation and negotiation are part of this process, but typically there is a direct interaction between the vendor (those doing the work) and the consumer (those paying for the work).

In an insurance claims scenario, the estimate is often sent to a representative of the insurance company as well as the customer. These parties usually have more developed layers of review and specific questions about the scope, cost, and/or duration of the project. The process can be tedious and time-consuming. There is a third party (the carrier) who has input and holds the majority of the purse strings.

In either scenario, as an estimator, you must focus on those items that are within your control, for example:

- Did I thoroughly capture the conditions from the worksite?
- Did I clearly communicate the scope of work in my estimate?
- Did I use my resources in a skilled way to support my plan?
- Did I do my best to anticipate questions and provide the information necessary to answer any objections or speculation?

Being willing to admit that a project outcome sucked is the first step in trying to identify those factors that contributed to the result.

In his article addressing decision-making for project managers, professor Randy R. Rapp makes this observation on the importance of discussing failures as a team,

> *"For some firms, it may simply be that defensiveness trumps the trust and honesty that might lead to better decisions. This is especially unfortunate since the sharp professional*

judgment characteristic of competent PMs probably develops more from recognizing and correcting prior sub-optimal decision-making than from any other single mechanism[8]."

Said another way, we often learn more from our losses than our wins. As we will discuss throughout this book and in the final Module, a key challenge of a healthy team is to create an environment where team members can share and receive constructive criticism. If we all want to improve, whether that is to no longer suck at estimating or to turn the corner on project outcomes that are inconsistent, we have to face ourselves with honesty.

Estimating is both an art and a science. In this book, I will attempt to help you sharpen your skills so that you can develop the mindset and habits that will elevate you and your organization above the status quo.

If you want different results, you will need to face some hard truths, including the reality that what got you here may not be what you need to get to the next level.

In his book, *Designed to Scale*, Lex Sisney shares his research and process for helping businesses adapt their mindsets to achieve their next-level goals. Lex shares that unless we make these internal changes as people in a position of leadership or as aspiring professionals, we will not see the changes that we need because they won't happen by themselves.

"Inertia essentially means that things tend to keep on doing what they've been doing until acted upon by a force of change...As a leader, where should you place your finite time and energy to create the most leverage to enact a force of change[9]?"

You will need to bring forces strong enough to counter the

[8] Rapp, R (2002, August) *Easy (?) Decision-Making.* Cost Engineering, Vol. 44/No. 8

[9] Sisney, L (2022) *Designed to Scale: How To Structure Your Business For Exponential Growth*

natural human bend towards accepting "good enough." If you want to rise above the status quo, you MUST inventory your current mindset and habits.

What do you need to **STOP** doing so that you are not working against yourself?

What do you need to **START** doing to take intentional steps towards your goals?

Guiding Principles

Like most restorers, the force that drew you to this industry is your desire to help people "make it better." Reading this book and taking this course represents your ongoing commitment to better yourself and your processes. We call this being an **Intentional Restorer**. If you are going to improve, and/or dumb down, your estimating process, you will need to develop core principles that you can translate to all of your team members.

We are going to identify and incorporate a guiding principle, *The Standard,* into our process improvement. While we will discuss some of the technical elements of estimating, in my experience, it's important to first lay a solid foundation for the **mindsets** and **habits** that will lead to better insurance claims outcomes. Too many people want to shortcut their learning curve, what we hope to accomplish is to help you shorten your DANG learning curve.

As it relates to the building blocks of better project outcomes, let's associate them with the scope of work that you are doing.

Water Damage Mitigation

If you are going to successfully complete a water damage mitigation project, what two things do you need to know?

You need to know **the source** of the damage and confirm that it has been addressed.

If you do not fix the source of the moisture issue, it will return. No one wins if the source isn't addressed properly. Knowing the source also informs your team on the category of water, as outlined in the IICRC S500 Standard for Professional Water Damage. The category of water affects safety as well as the scope of work, therefore it impacts how the estimate should be written to include these cost considerations.

> The next thing you need to know is **the extent** of the damages.

We use various tools as well as our five senses to monitor building materials and determine how far the moisture traveled throughout the structure. The extent of the damages and the details of the structural composition affect the class of water. Class of water informs elements of our response that affect the scope, cost, and duration of the project. When you know the source and the extent you can begin to formulate your game plan and put it into action.

Reconstruction (repairs)

Similarly, if you are preparing a scope of work for repairs it's helpful to know where the loss originated from (source).

As an estimator, you will want to confirm whoever performed the dry-out did so properly by addressing the source and extent of damages so that your team doesn't inherit the liability for unresolved issues. In order to complete the repairs, you need to address any structural elements prior to moving forward with anything else. Working side by side with the mitigation team as well as observing or helping with reconstruction are helpful in expanding your estimating abilities.

Having some guiding principles around scope capture is helpful for every team member. Robert Harrell, adjuster turned contractor turned software specialist, shares that there are <u>four key elements of a solid scope</u>:

Element 1: Product Name or Identification (ex. drywall)
Element 2: Quality (ex. 1/2 - smooth coat finish)
Element 3: Quantity (ex. 96 square feet)
Element 4: Repair Methodology (ex. remove and replace)

In practice, these four elements would lead the estimator, or anyone capturing project details, to consistently ask four questions:

Q1. What am I looking at?
A1. Flood damage wallboard

Q2. What are the qualities of the product?
A2. Half-inch drywall (½") with a smooth finish (level 5)

Q3. What are the quantities of the product?
A3. 48 linear feet (LF) long by 2 feet high = 96 square feet (SF) - 48' x 2'. If a sheet of drywall is 4' x 8' (32 SF), how many sheets will the team need?

Q4. What is the repair methodology?
A4. Remove and replace affected drywall

NOTE: In reality, my field notes might simply be, "B1 (Bedroom 1) R&R (remove and replace) 48 x 2 ½" smooth DRY."

In the "old days" companies were pretty proud of their exhaustive tick sheets, which often doubled as their pricing sheets. When the industry ran on carbon copy paper (look it up), a technician might enter a series of checkmarks next to typical work sequences to
ensure that they performed those tasks and that the billing department captured those revenue items.

An estimator might use something similar or compose scope notes in their own shorthand. It is important to capture site details in a systematic and consistent way so that those details can be shared in a clear and thorough manner.

- If you are an estimator and commonly miss items that affect your ability to write a complete scope…
- If you are a manager and your team members commonly miss items that lead to poor project outcomes…
- If you are an owner and are frustrated by low profit margins…

…it is time to create and hold team members accountable to the consistent practice of thorough data capture (TDC) which we will address in Module 3. Tick Sheets, work sequences, and standard operating procedures (SOPs) still have their role in a thriving organization. Groups like *KnowHow*[10] have helped innovate methods for providing integrated and accessible processes for your team.

Many of the job management software options developed within our industry have some of these items built into their platforms as well. If your company isn't doing this, as an estimator or aspiring professional, it is helpful for you personally to have a checklist of common items to ensure you capture all of the details.

If you are learning to estimate, print out the line items from Xactimate and look at the default macros within the program. Macros are line item lists related to a scope of work. They can be created by you, purchased from outlets such as Actionable Insights, or found within Xactimate.

As an organization, it is important to create clarity, consistency, and accountability in all of your key service lines. If you want to scale and grow your business, your team members need to know the WHAT and the WHY of your unique way of doing business (vision and values). This starts with the most basic element, clarifying what the universal standard is (or should be) for all insurance claims projects.

The Claims Standard

---

[10] Tryknowhow.com

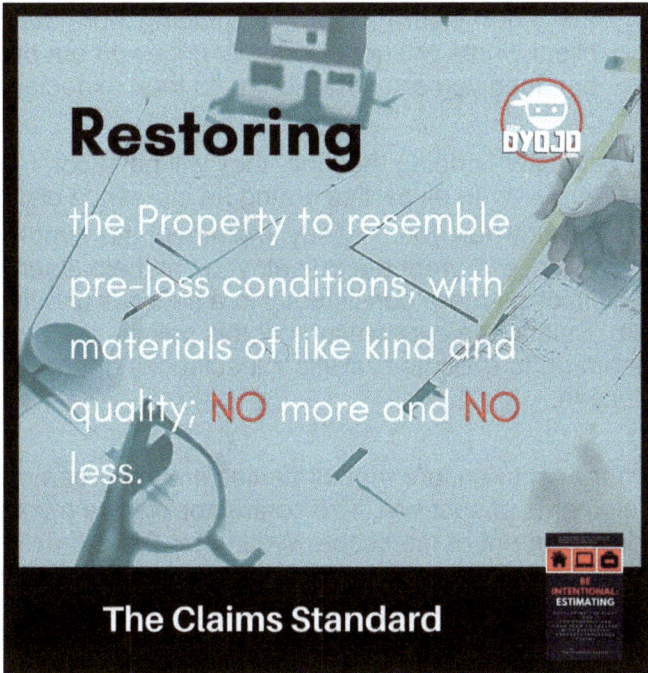

Restoring

the Property to resemble pre-loss conditions, with materials of like kind and quality; NO more and NO less.

The Claims Standard

We said we were going to add a guiding principle to our growing arsenal for better project outcomes, so here it is:

The Claims Standard: *Restoring the property to resemble pre-loss conditions, with materials of like kind and quality; no more and no less.*

Your initial site inspection <u>identifies</u> the affected areas related to the source and extent of the damages. As you develop the scope, you need to <u>clarify</u> what <u>is</u> and <u>is not</u> part of the

agreed-upon scope of work. You may <u>discover</u> areas of additional damage, but you need to be clear about whether these are issues your team is responsible to address.

For an insurance claim, doing more than what the policy owes and attempting to charge the carrier for it (i.e. "maximizing the claim") is fraud.

For a non-insurance project, bidding more than what the client wants will unnecessarily price you out of a job because you are not listening to their expectations.

If the estimator is doing their job, they will have communicated *The Standard*[11] to all parties during an insurance claim.

I believe that when you properly implement this simple narrative into your process, from the outset, you can help steer the project lifecycle more consistently to a successful outcome (habit). Setting the expectations at this point in the project sets the team up to execute realistic expectations during production.

Do your best to ensure that all parties are in agreement on the key elements of success. The contractor plays a pivotal role in the development of the scope. Writing for Claims Journal, attorney Gary Wickert reiterates the importance of a through site visit and an accurate estimate from a qualified local contractor:

> *"The policy should pay for the cost of an experienced contractor to perform the required work to repair or replace the building and **put it back to its pre-loss condition**."*

We all believe the policy should do this, but how is the scpe and cost formed Gary explains,

> *"Insurance companies use guideline pricing and "Xactimate" (computerized home replacement cost estimating software) to predict how much materials and labor should cost."*

Estimating software helps to formulate and predict costs, but does the carrier or the software have the final say on these matters?

---

[11] Isaacson, J. (2021, May 5) *The Mindset and Habits for Claims Estimating Success as a New Independent Adjuster.* Claims Pages. https://www.claimspages.com/editorials/2021/05/05/the-mindset-and-habits-for-claims-estimating-success-as-a-new-independent-adjuster

"The estimate prepared by a qualified local, licensed, and bonded contractor who has visited the loss site and reviewed information about the pre-loss structure is generally the most accurate cost for a claim settlement[12]."

The later sections of this book will deal more with Xactimate. Our focus in this module are guiding principles. In Module 3 we will address the **scope** (of the work) as well as how we determine the appropriate **cost** (of the work). When you properly document the site conditions, record quality measurements, and compose detailed notes, you have the building blocks to draft a defensible estimate.

A critical conversation you must have as a leadership team is ensuring everyone understands their roles and responsibilities as it relates to The Standard.

To the owner/manager

Accountability for outcomes can only be established when the process is clear and the follow through is consistent.

Clarity + Consistency = Accountability.

You can help your organization grow by being honest about whether your system is dumb by design (revealing intentionality) or whether negative outcomes are the by-product of dumb design. If the project outcomes are inconsistent, a great place to start with whether you have been clear and consistent. You can look at this as dumbing down the process so that someone who has no industry experience can understand what they need to do and why it is important to the team.

You are responsible for clearly and consistently communicating as well as training your team on The Standard. As Intentional Restorers, this ethic should guide all that we do. It is important in this process to clarify the roles and responsibilities of the customer, the contractor, and the carrier. Our friends at Super

---

[12] Wickert, G (2019, October 31) *Paying Overhead and Profit in First-Party Claims.* Claims Journal. https://www.claimsjournal.com/columns/road-to-recovery/2019/10/31/293871.htm

Tech University[13] have created a robust library of daily training videos to help your team develop their soft skills because it is as important for your team to know **what to say** as it is to learn **how to say it**.

To the estimator

There are some clear lines and some gray areas that are involved in what we should and should not be doing as contractors. A clear line is fraud. We should not be a party to fraud. We should not be aiding a customer to "maximize" a claim without justification from the structural damage observed or the conditions of the damage event (*no more*). We also should not be a party to "minimizing" costs without a value-added proposition that is transparent and agreed to by all parties (*no less*). We do not want the carrier and the customer teaming up against us, so we should not be colluding with either party against the other. The contractor plays an important role in The Restoration Triangle.

To the aspiring professional

Assuming your company wants to "do things the right way", or whatever variation they have incorporated into their vision and values, it should reflect The Standard. If you can do it right, you will set yourself apart from other aspiring professionals in your field. When a technician moves to a new company, there often is some element of culture shock as well as confusion with regards to a new (to them) "right way" to do things.

Some companies pride themselves on saying, "Forget what you learned with Team X and buckle in as you learn Team Y's Way of doing things." This can be confusing because your frame of reference is what you learned from Team X. I had a conversation with a technician recently who was struggling with this issue. I shared,

> *If they are investing in their people, that's a good sign.*

---

[13] https://morningtechmeeting.com/

If they have a different way, that's not necessarily wrong. There are many ways to do everything. Before you assume this new way is wrong, ask them to explain to you in better detail how it works. Unless it violates the law or sound ethics, give it 90 days and see what you learn.

If they are saying, 'Do this because it will make us more money,' this is not always the best approach but it isn't inherently wrong. Find out what the process is and why they do it. People can do the right thing for the wrong reasons as well as the wrong thing for the right reasons. Our goal is always to do the right things for the right reasons, but there can be a lot of gray areas.

Unfortunately, not every manager or owner is able to distinguish between an earnest inquiry and an obstinate employee. If you are a technician, you should ask questions if you want to grow. You need to discern when you are being directed to do something and when or how to best go about asking your questions.

Within your intentional estimating toolbag you now have:
- The Claims Standard

Module 1 Quiz

1. What is *The Standard* for insurance claims presented in this module?

2. What two questions do you need to answer for every project
- *what is the* _____ *of the loss, and what is the*
_____ *of the damages?*

3. What are the <u>four key elements of a solid scope</u>:

Element 1:
Element 2:
Element 3:
Element 4:

4. What is The DYOJO Way?

Do It _____
Do it _____
Do it _____

Additional Resources

Mindset and habits for insurance claims estimating - read *Be Intentional: Estimating* - http://thedyojo.com/book1

If you don't want to read the whole book, read the article that lead to the book - *The 10 Commandments of Xactimate Estimating Success* published in R&R Magazine - https://www.randrmagonline.com/articles/88186-the-10-commandments-of-xactimate-estimating-success

Watch *The Xactimate Sessions* from The DYOJO Podcast, **Episode 1** discusses learning insurance claims estimating with no prior background in the restoration industry - https://www.youtube.com/watch?v=EN2k2Gb4Yrw&t=1312s

Check out the amazing courses offered by the team at **Restoration Technical Institute** (RTI) - https://rtilearning.com/

The author with Pete Consigili, RIA 2022
- Photo credit Ed Cross

Module Two

A Good Sketch Is A Good Start

As an aspiring professional, there should be no shame in admitting that you [currently] suck. If you want to grow your career, develop your team, and improve your project outcomes, it is good to admit that you suck and to recognize the importance of design in improving your process. You may not have a leadership role that allows you to speak into the design of the organization, but you have so many resources at your fingertips to help you educate and elevate your industry knowledge.

Have you heard the phrase, "First, do no harm?" You likely have attributed it to the *Hippocratic Oath* which is supposed to be the guiding principle for medical professionals. According to the National Institutes of Health, this oath signified the early stages of medical training, calling new physicians to swear to uphold a number of **voluntary professional ethical standards**. Pay attention to this segment and see how many of the elements aptly apply to the services provided by property restoration contractors:

> *"Into whatever homes I go, I will enter them for the benefit of the sick, avoiding any voluntary act of impropriety or corruption. So long as I maintain this Oath faithfully and without corruption, may it be granted to me to partake of life fully and the practice of my art, gaining the respect of all men for all time[14]."*

In 2007, the Association of Specialists in Cleaning and Restoration (ASCR) rebranded as the Restoration Industry Association (RIA). At that time the group unveiled the first motto of their 60-year history, *"We make it better. We promise[15]."*

[14] National Institutes of Health (2002, September 16 *Greek Medicine: The Hippocratic Oath*. https://www.nlm.nih.gov/hmd/greek/greek_oath.html

[15] Consigli, P. & Zlotnik, C. (2017, October 26) *Connecting Mission With Motto.* Cleaning & Restoration. https://www.restorationindustry.org/cleaning-and-restoration/connecting-mission-motto

Simple and concise, which is a good general rule for anything that we would consider as a guiding principle.

We are professionals, in so far as we educate ourselves on and adhere to industry best practices. We make it better, when we serve the client in restoring the structure to its pre-loss condition, or better in the event that they elect to pay for upgrades (we will discuss this distinction in greater detail in Module 3). We may not heal sick human bodies, but we are **Doctors of Disaster** treating damaged structures. If we are going to "make it better," our process must include measures to ensure that we:

- Properly identify the extent of the damages
- Prevent cross-contamination
- Thoroughly address structural impacts
- Restore the property to resemble pre-loss conditions.

The quality of your service, and that of your team, will be in proportion to the level of effort you put into learning and implementing industry standards. If you aim to be a Doctor of Disaster you must seek out and implement:

Voluntary standards that help to educate intentional restorers on how to do the work the **right** way.

Tools such as this course that assist intentional restorers in doing things **efficiently**.

Best practices that help intentional restorers do things **excellently**.

Growing as a professional and as an organization is a lifelong pursuit. As we gain new information and apply it, we become wiser and better in our roles and responsibilities. As we learn to suck less, sometimes we uncomfortably have to face where we have been sucking all along.

Get a group of restoration owners and managers together, and what are some of the challenges they share in common with each other? High on the list will be getting team members to consistently and thoroughly complete their documentation. In my various content platforms, I continually share, "We get paid for what we document." The caveat may be, "And even that can be a challenge." Documentation is vital.

If you are an aspiring professional, your company owner and managers want you to understand that you all shoot yourselves in the foot when you don't have quality documentation. If you want to advance in your career, start here - do your DANG paperwork. As you advance in this industry or most others, there is never less documentation; it's always more. So, you can't say that you want to climb the ladder while refusing to master the key steps of your current position. **What you are doing now matters.**

I wrote an article for Restoration and Remediation (R&R) Magazine, titled *The 10 Commandments of Xactimate Estimating Success*[16], which was the most viewed of 2018. When Michelle Blevins, now the owner of Cleaning and Restoration (C&R) Magazine shared the news with me, I thought this demonstrated that there was a need and interest in the industry to expand on the subject of mindset and habits for estimating success. This effort led to publishing my first moderately selling book, *Be Intentional: Estimating*.

Moving from the realm of the status quo to the realm of the intentional isn't complicated. Quite the opposite, the path is simple but that doesn't mean it is easy. Jack Nicklaus, the famous golfer framed this mindset well when he said, *"Talent isn't as important as the work and dedication necessary to become competent."* If you want to improve, there is no shortcut, you have to put the work in.

In the last module we discussed how you need to identify two key elements for mitigating damages:

- What is the source of the damage?
- What is the extent of the damage?

---

[16] Isaacson, J (2018 September 17) *The 10 Commandments of Xactimate Estimating Success.* R&R Magazine.
https://www.randrmagonline.com/articles/88186-the-10-commandments-of-xactimate-estimating-success

As we translate that information into an estimate or an invoice, we need two primary pieces of documentation:

- A good sketch is a good start
- You can never take too many photos

During a surge of freeze losses in Eugene, Oregon, I learned that as long as I had a *decent* diagram and some *decent* photos, I could duct tape a *decent* estimate together. As a manager, you may have said, "Garbage-in leads to garbage-out," when chastising your field staff. But, have you ever stepped back to review your client intake process and the details that you provide your first response teams with when they go to a new loss? Garbage-in, Garbage-out applies to owners, managers, and intake processes as well.

During that freeze, we were taking in more claims than we had the people power to respond to, so we streamlined our process. Our teams were able to get the key details that helped us to capture and input the majority of the details. We learned a lot about the gaps in our system when it was tested beyond its maximum capacity.

Fast forward to now. I am approached by companies, most often contractors who are having an issue with their first insurance claim, or restoration contractors who are struggling with their estimating process, and the greatest struggle is to get the project details from the owner or management staff. Documentation must flow top-down as well as bottom-up. It's a process and it is the responsibility of every team member.

Estimating is a team effort. If you want to achieve better project outcomes, you have to continually train and improve your whole process.

If you struggle to get the details from your technicians:

- Have them spend a day with an estimator so that they can see how the process works. The opposite is true as it is important for estimators to understand how hard your technicians work and what it takes to get the work that they are bidding done.

- Cross-train them on the fundamental elements of estimating. Help team members connect their current responsibilities with opportunities for advancing their careers.
- Be sure that you are looking at your documentation process as a whole, which starts with client intake (be consistent).

Sketching Habits

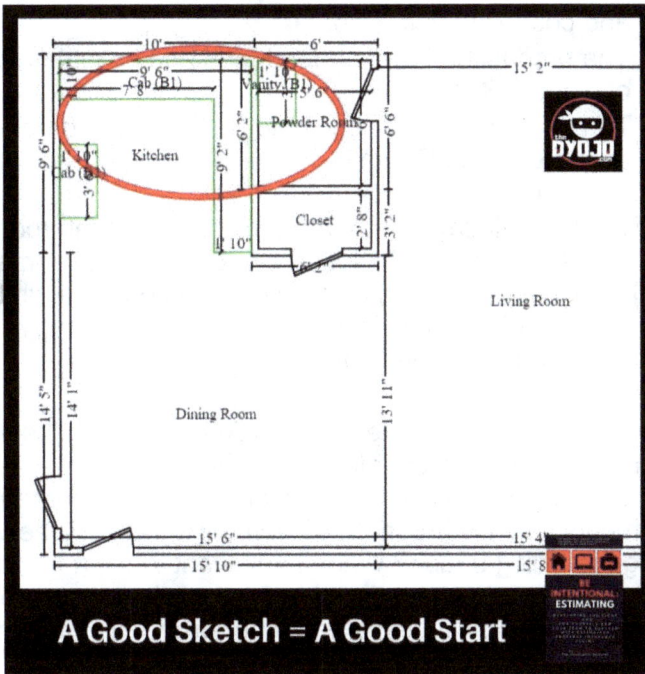

A Good Sketch = A Good Start

There has been so much innovation and integration of technology, even in the short period of time between when I first wrote the *10 Commandments* article in 2018 and now. If your team is not experimenting with technology to make your processes more efficient I fear for your sustainability. For the majority of claims, a detailed and to-scale worksite diagram is the expectation. Having this accurate sketch helps you communicate consistently with the customer, the carrier, and your production teams. The larger the project, the more helpful it is to have a map of the worksite.

What is the difference between a living room and a family room or a dining room and a formal dining room? While the definitions matter, what matters to the estimate, the agreed-upon scope, the contract, and the production plan are what those documents have consistently defined them to be. If the room with the toilet in it next to the kitchen was called Room 4, then for all of the integrated systems that follow, it is Room 4.

- The estimate notes the damages and/or repairs in Room 4
- The adjuster and the customer have agreed to the scope and cost of work in Room 4
- The production team understands and executes the scope of work in Room 4
- The company bills and is paid for the work completed and documented in Room 4

We can argue all day whether that room was a bathroom, ½ bath, powder room, wash closet, etc. But what really matters is that the communication is clear and consistent through the life cycle of the project so we can regularly achieve happy customers and profitable jobs.

Conversely, if the estimate calls out Room 4 (because the estimator was lazy in their labeling), the customer calls it the ½ bath, the adjuster calls it the powder room, and your team documents it as Bathroom 2, do you think there will be issues during the billing phase? What if you went to court for some reason? Do you think the lawyers for the other team are going to have a field day picking this and other discrepancies apart in your scope?

Whether you use Xactimate or not, a job site diagram is helpful to all parties involved. A sketch of the project helps us to identify the layout of the structure and speak in a common language about WHERE we are and WHAT we are doing in specific areas. A quality sketch will help us to derive simple calculations such as square footage (SF) of a room, cubic feet (CF) of space, and linear feet (LF) of materials.

In Xactimate, there are several helpful calculations that can be quickly derived from a quality sketch. Many contractors do not use the tool to its potential yet blame it for being the bane of their existence. If I cannot drive a nail properly, do I blame the hammer? No, the hammer is just a tool. Likewise, Xactimate, or any other estimating software, is a tool. If you want to use the tool effectively, you will be consistently learning new means and methods to optimize your use of that tool through experience and training.

In my experience, personal opinion, and ongoing practice, ¼" by ¼" graph paper is the gold standard of job site sketching. Even if you use current innovations, which I recommend, you should start with a pen, paper, and laser tape measure. It's important to know the foundational tools, to **do it right**, before you initiate innovation, to **do it efficiently**. When your technology glitches you need to know how to get the job done.

I created a video[17] outlining what was then high tech, tape measure and lined paper vs. laser measure and graph paper. My young children were my test subjects and I taught them the basic principles of diagraming a room. I think these disciplines still hold up as you train technicians[18], new project managers, and estimators. Before you can teach someone to sketch in Xactimate, or any other platform, they need to understand how to diagram a structure the "old school" way.

A Few Sketch (Diagram) Habits

- One simple tip for sketching is to always start your sketch at the corner of two exterior walls. If you start from the center you will create a sketch that won't line up or will need secondary pages.
- The second tip is to use a scale in proportion to the project. I usually use ¼" = 2' or for smaller projects ¼" = 1'.
- Always measure and mark your doors, cabinets, damaged areas, fixtures, etc.
- It is helpful to utilize color for certain common scopes of work such as red for flood cut areas, orange for flooring removed, green for cabinets, etc.

---

[17] Improving your Xactimate estimates through better claims sketches
https://www.youtube.com/watch?v=2h7TKRh__Ho&t=9s

[18] Isaacson, J (2021, August 9) *Training Restoration Technicians to Sketch for Xactimate.* R&R Magazine. https://www.randrmagonline.com/articles/89524-training-restoration-technicians-to-sketch-for-xactimate

In Module 5, I will demonstrate four common estimating approaches. Using a simple drywall repair I will show how understanding the scope of work and learning to more fully utilize the capabilities of your estimating software can lead to a clearer path to profitability. Keith Nelson, Senior Commercial Project Consultant, reminds restorers that there is always a place for the 'old school' ways,

"To this day, I believe I measure old school and enter the sketch myself in the time it takes to get a Matterport scan and sketch sent to me. It is my fear that as an industry we are losing the personal touch to technology. It is also my fear that the next generation will not even know what a tape measure is."

Can You Take Too Many Photos?

The answer is no, you cannot take too many photographs for an insurance claims project. Nor can you take too many before, progress, and after photos for any project in the skilled trades. This was true even when restorers were taking photos with leading technology the likes of:

- Stone tablets
- Polaroid cameras that slowly printed photos onsite
- Rolls of 35mm film that captured up to 36 photos and took 24 hours (or more) to process
- When Sony came out with the Mavica, it was a game-changer by storing photos on a 3.5" floppy disc that you could download to your computer
- The dawn of the digital camera, clunky units that didn't take quality pictures or have good storage capabilities
- Smartphones that put low-quality photographic technology at our fingertips

Each of these advancements helped intentional restorers to do their job just a little bit more efficiently. In the modern age of high-quality images with relatively inexpensive technology and cloud-based storage options, there literally is no excuse for lackluster documentation.

I don't understand why some industry professionals resist sharing their sketches[19], ESX, photos, or 360-degree imaging. I would rather all parties were working from my documentation. I can understand protecting your investment and agree that you should create provisions for charging for your time as well as the resources allocated to these efforts.

Many contractors either charge for inspections, get a work authorization signed prior to the delivery of the estimate or utilize customer qualifying tools such as a letter of intent (LOI). Whatever you do, make sure you have clear and consistent communication with your client on the process and expectations. Advantages of contractors sharing their documentation adapted from my article in *Property Casualty 360*

- Technology has created avenues to expand the reach and consolidate resources for all parties to a claim.
- If an adjuster and a contractor are negotiating a claim, they can both access the scanning resource and discuss claims
- items with the benefit of a three-dimensional room-by-room review.
- When an adjuster or restorer sits down to write their damage estimate, having the 360-degree capture open at the same time will help to jog their memory as well as provide them with another view of the structural conditions.
- If we want to arrive at an expedited, agreed-upon scope of work that is as accurate and thorough as possible, everyone in the claims chain will benefit from having access to the same information.

---

[19] Isaacson, J (2022, January 7) *How does 360 scanning help expedite claims processing?* Property Casualty 360.
https://www.propertycasualty360.com/2022/01/07/how-does-360-scanning-help-expedite-claims-processing/

Structuring Your Photos

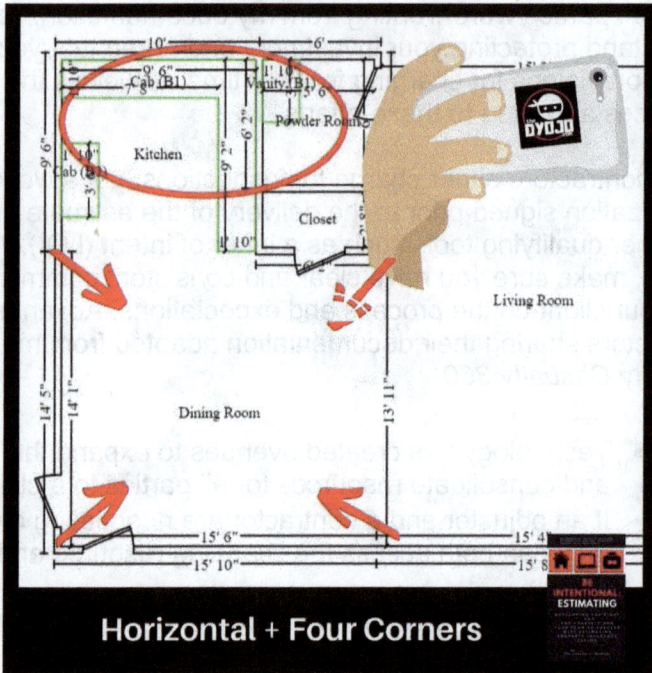

Horizontal + Four Corners

Rachel Adams-Beja phrases it well when she says, "You can never have too much documentation unless it's wrong." While you cannot take too many photos, you definitely can take photos that are difficult to utilize in any meaningful way.

Owners and managers should be clear and consistent in how they train their team members to utilize technology. You cannot expect something, like consistent quality photo documentation, without investing in regular training. Don't assume that people know what you want or need, show them the way. If you are upset with the consistency and quality of the documentation, it's on you to change those habits. Estimators play a role in setting the tone for the team as well.

Often poor attitudes and habits can be a reflection of an incomplete process rollout. For example, I can remember onboarding a new technology that our corporate office said was going to simplify everything and it was a pain in the butt to use. The organization was committed to the product, so we all had to work together to figure out how to make it work for our local office.

You may not go to the extreme of Undercover Boss like a few CEOs in our industry, but you should try the systems yourself before you chastise your team members for their lack of compliance. *When was the last time you went into the field with your team members and documented a loss using your systems to upload the information?*

A Few Photo Habits

Everything you do is about communication. Most often you are communicating the scope to claims professionals who likely will not set foot on the project. The clearer and more consistent you are in your process of thorough data capture, the more effective you will be in your ability to accurately communicate the story of

the loss (data input). You accomplish this through photos, line items, and scope notes.

If you learn to improve and master your ability to speak in a common language you will increase your ability to achieve better claims outcomes.

- You should always take your photos, presumably with your phone, horizontally rather than vertically
- Start your photo process by taking a panoramic view from the four corners of each affected room
- Take before, during, and after photos
- Photos should be labeled to provide clarity on the context of what room they were taken from and what they are demonstrating to the reviewer
- Take close-up photos of specific damages
- The higher the value of the affected item, the more photos
- If you are photographing contents or detailed scopes, number markers are helpful as reference points
- Do everyone a favor and take a video walkthrough to give an overview of the project - make note of the source, the affected areas, and unique aspects of the

scope that someone might otherwise miss if they weren't physically onsite

How many times have you observed a job site photograph and wondered, "What the heck am I looking at?" Imagine how confused the adjuster or reviewer will be if there are no labels providing context for your submitted photos. When the documentation you gather (data capture) and the information that you share with the customer and/or the carrier (data input) are not in sync with each other, you are shooting yourself and your team in the foot.

A picture is worth a thousand words. But, what good will it do you if you take a thousand photos and none of them are in context?

If you put the work into making a good diagram with your rooms/areas defined (labeled), your photographs and all corresponding documentation should utilize these same reference points.

Document. Document. Then document some more (The Three D's).

You reduce a lot of time and confusion by labeling photos from the worksite. This is one of the reasons I enjoy using DocuSketch. In that program whoever is taking the photo (aka "Comment") is entering a description that is already labeled according to the room name. The same applies when utilizing remote estimators, whether that is an internal resource or you send your estimates to another company that specializes in that service. Quality labeled photos are key. What if the extreme occurs and you find yourself in litigation? Ask our good friend Ed Cross, The Restoration Lawyer, how important clear, abundant, and easy to reference documentation is.

To the aspiring professional

It is to your benefit to learn all you can so that you can be the best you are able in your current role. This raises your credibility when you want to promote and it provides you with a solid fall-back plan. For a business, there is such a thing as growing too fast; the same is true for individuals. When you grow faster than

your ability to lay a strong foundation and develop the resources to succeed, you will struggle and likely fail. Advancing too fast can be as dangerous as waiting too
long. Your personal development in soft skills (people and leadership) is as important as your technical skills if you want to be promoted.

You can learn <u>what to do</u> from good managers, but you will have to learn to adapt those lessons to your way of accomplishing your role and responsibilities.

Even though bad managers are a drain on your experiences, they can also teach you <u>what not to do</u>. Both are valuable lessons and everyone can teach you something if you are willing to learn.

To the estimator

While team members and managers may be upset about the quality or accuracy of estimates, it is important to remember that an estimate by definition is not a finished product. Many contractors are hesitant to write change orders, but amendments to the scope and cost should be understood as a normal function of the process. I believe one of the greatest areas of improvement, for property restoration contractors especially, is in the communication between teams rather than casting blame for negative outcomes.

In his presentation *Is Estimating Accuracy An Oxymoron?* Larry Dysert identified several factors affecting estimating accuracy which included:

- Quality of reference cost estimating data (material pricing, labor hours, labor wage rates, etc.)
- Quality of assumptions used in preparing the estimate
- State of technology in the project
- Experience and skill level of the estimator
- Level of effort budgeted to prepare the estimate
- Market conditions (periods of rapid price escalation and labor climate factors)

These items speak to the importance of the process leading up to estimate composition, which includes technology, the time and/or effort budgeted to focus on the estimate, and the data (documentation) provided. If the estimating process is focused on quantity over quality, the end product will reflect this.

You know you need a good sketch and quality-labelled photos. Have you experimented with some of the technologies that help you make your time onsite more efficient? Partner with and cross-train your team members so that they can better understand and help your team to be successful. Look for opportunities to roll your sleeves up and keep yourself familiar with the work. Use your voice to advocate for the team members that are working their butts off to help you look awesome.

To the owner/manager

Wherever possible, make your team's job easier. Provide them with the tools that help them to help you. Sometimes this means you experiment with items that don't work or quickly become outdated. Cross-train your teams both to increase their appreciation for each other's roles and to help team members comprehend what they need to do if they want to advance in your organization.

Within your intentional estimating toolbag you now have:
- The Claims Standard
- A To-Scale Sketch and Numerous Labeled Photos

Module 3 Quiz

1. Complete the sentence, a good _____, is a _____ start.

2. Common sketch abbreviations
   LF =
   SF =
   CF =

3. What happens when you are not consistent with naming (labeling) and referring to rooms in a project diagram?

4. What are some of the keys to consistently taking quality photographic documentation for your insurance claim estimates?

Additional Resources

Where do you start when learning to sketch for insurance claims estimating? Watch this **video** - *Improving your Xactimate estimates through better claims sketches* - https://www.youtube.com/watch?v=2h7TKRh__Ho&t=9s

Read **the article** *How does 360 scanning help expedite claims processing?* Published in Property Casualty 360 - https://www.propertycasualty360.com/2022/01/07/how-does-360-scanning-help-expedite-claims-processing/

Watch **the video** for The DYOJO Podcast Episode 40 discussing the use of Docusketch with two restorers, an adjuster, and a representative of the company - https://www.youtube.com/watch?v=1b-AVqz59Q8

Watch **the video** *Improving As An Xactimate Estimator* from our series The Xactimate Sessions - https://www.youtube.com/watch?v=cejyebuPkVI&t=848s

The DYOJO Scoping Diagram, Pt. 1

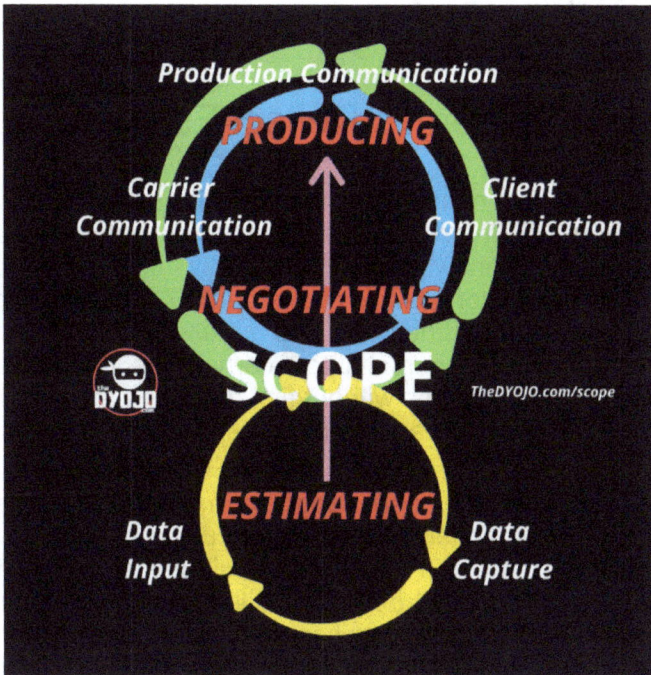

Module Three

Project Outcomes Reflect Estimate Inputs

When you arrive onsite, what two questions does every customer ask? Before you have even rolled out your tape measure, the client wants to know, "How much is this going to cost?" and "How long is this going to take?" The order may be interchangeable but the questions are always the same. Be careful not to paint yourself into a corner by attempting to answer those questions without first gathering the information you need to generate an informed response.

I think much of the modern consumer mentality is shaped by home improvement shows. What the customer expects is that we can walk through a house in five minutes or less and tell them, "This will cost $1,500 (seems like this is the magic number for everything) and my crew can start this afternoon." Unfortunately this is not how things work in the real world. If you need to prove this to a client, you can find stories like this one from **Fast Company** that reveal these shows are selling "fantasy at best and nightmare at worst".

> *"While many consumers focus on the price, in the world of insurance claims property restoration the scope is the foundational element[20]."*

You know that the expectations of the consumer typically are not in alignment with reality and they hardly ever will be. Your challenge as a contractor is to create a scope, cost, and duration that will lead to a happy customer and profitable project completion. When a customer wants us to answer those two questions, you can start the education process with The Standard and the four phases of an insurance claims estimate:

---

[20] Brownlee, J (2016, April 19) *Here's Why You Should Never Go On A Reality Home Renovation Show.* Fast Company. https://www.fastcompany.com/3059083/heres-why-you-should-never-go-on-a-reality-home-renovation-show

Phase 1: Observe and document the conditions of the damaged property (TDC). Compose and communicate the proposed scope and the estimated cost (ADI) to the customer and/or the carrier.

Phase 2: Answer questions from the customer and/or the carrier about the scope of work that we have proposed, i.e. review and revisions.

Phase 3: Create a contract based upon the agreed-upon scope and cost of the work.

Phase 4: Clarify any **supplements** (those changes being submitted to the carrier for consideration with the claim) and **change orders** (those changes being submitted to the customer for work and/or upgrades not specifically part of the claim), especially those that impact the start or continuation of work.

When a customer wants to get the process started as soon as possible, we explain that we can create a contract based on our price but they will be responsible for any variance between our estimated cost and what the insurance agrees to pay. Some contractors refuse to work with the carrier, positioning themselves to only work for and with the customer.

In a mitigation scenario, it is useful to help the customer understand what the carrier likely will approve (undisputed amount) and the reason for the delta between your invoice. If they agreed from the project onset that they were contracting directly with you and paying for the work, stick with that. If you agreed to "roll the dice" on some portion of the scope and cost, you will have to work through that.

In a repairs scenario, the same can be true, educate the client and set realistic expectations on the scope and cost. The options for the customer may include 1) agree to our total scope, cost, and the responsibility for any variance, 2) agree to what we believe is the undisputed amount or phase 1 (i.e. items such as insulation and drywall) while we wait for confirmation on the other items, or 3) wait until everything is confirmed with the insurance company and proceed from there.

There should be a level of transparency and education as we are the professionals who do this day-in and day-out. The customer should not be surprised by outcomes if we are working as their ally in the restoration process. Scope and cost should be clear to all parties. If the customer is responsible to pay any amount out of pocket, how much and why should be clear to them.

Estimating is the process of establishing the agreed-upon scope and cost for a given project. As contractors, we utilize a simple estimating formula to guide our process:

Thorough Data Capture (TDC) +
Accurate Data Input (ADI) =
A Defensible Estimate (ADE)

If you are struggling to produce consistently positive project outcomes, you should review whether your data inputs (estimate) are accurate as well as whether your data capture (documentation) is thorough. You must take accountability for this truth:

The quality of the data inputs (composed estimate)
is in direct correlation to the quality of the data captured.

Everyone on the team should understand the importance of gathering and sharing quality documentation from the worksite. The reader will recall the four elements of identifying scope from Module One - Description, Quality, Quantity, and Strategy. We combine all of those elements (data capture) together to create *the story of the loss* (data input).

A Simple Estimating Formula

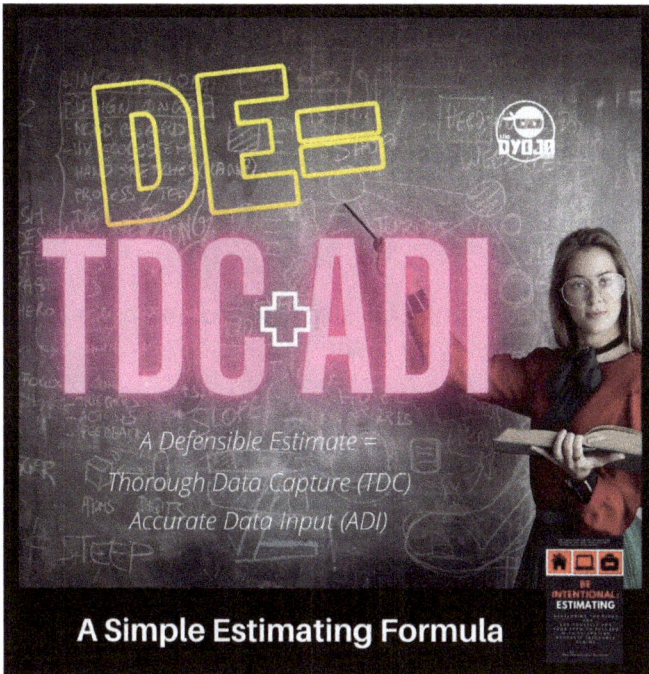

A Defensible Estimate =
Thorough Data Capture (TDC)
Accurate Data Input (ADI)

A Simple Estimating Formula

Thorough Data Capture

An insurance claim is a unique process whereby the customer hires a contractor to perform work that the carrier is primarily paying for. The data capture phase is vital to setting yourself up for success in writing a good estimate which in turn is vital to setting your team up for success to understand and execute on the agreed-upon scope. As an estimator, you will do everyone a favor by making the previously mentioned Standard clear at the outset of every claim. Your introduction could be something to the effect of,

"My job is to perform thorough data capture of the site conditions so that I can accurately data input to generate an estimate for an agreed-upon scope (most likely through Xactimate) to restore your property to resemble pre-loss conditions."

Whoever is inspecting the affected worksite will need to develop and/or follow a process that aids them to capture the following:

Quality diagram (sketch) with clear room labels +

Quality photos that are clearly labeled +

Quality estimate, written in the flow of the work, with clear scope notes =

Quality opportunity for all parties to be on the same page during the life cycle of the project

The contract forms the agreement between the customer and the contractor. The contract is based on the agreed-upon scope and cost of the work to be performed. Once the customer contracts with the restorer, making them the contractor of record, they have the responsibility to act in the best interests of their client (the insured). Pete Consigli, the Global Restoration Watchdog, states that mastery and success in this role include,

"The contractor's good faith effort to act in their client's best interests, make a profit, and not alienate the insurance adjuster."

It is important that the contractor or the insured do not conflate the meaning of "the best interests of the client" to mean something other than *The Standard*.

Contractor > Scope & Cost > Contract

The contractor should be very clear on what is and is not part of the approved scope as it relates to damages and repairs covered under the contract.

Adjuster > Coverage > Policy

The adjuster is responsible for explaining to the client what is and is not covered, or what is excluded, and supporting that by citing the policy.

It is important for the contractor to educate the client on these roles and to stay in their lane of competency. Contractors can do the wrong thing, such as attempting to interpret or advise on the insurance policy, for the right reasons, such as trying to help their customer. But doing the wrong thing for the right reason, is still the wrong thing, or an action that could put your company and your customer in a bad spot.

As our friend David Princeton, a licensed public adjuster who specializes in claims advocacy, advises contractors in his column **Dear David**,

> *"A contractor could be wise not to speak to coverage or the law. A potential warning sign of a line being crossed is reading the insurance policy. Some go further by interpreting its meaning and expressing an opinion about what the coverage should or should not do[21]."*

Again, note the areas of expertise and the guiding principles as it relates to the process of developing the agreed-upon scope and cost of the work:

> The contractor is responsible for the **scope** of repairs as outlined in the **contract**.

> The adjuster (or claims representative) is responsible to clarify the extent of **coverage** (including any clear exclusions) as outlined in the insurance **policy**.

> If you have been educating your client on The Standard and your process for presenting the story of the loss, the insured

[21] Princeton, D (2022, April 11) *Dear David: Why Does Doing The Right Thing Get Me In Trouble.* C&R Magazine. https://candrmagazine.com/dear-david-why-does-doing-the-right-thing-get-me-in-trouble/

should be empowered to participate in advocating for themselves to ensure the proper scope is approved. In our restoration business, we encourage all of our clients to keep detailed notes and their own documentation of the claims process. We are creating **videos to help**[22] set expectations and help those who have never experienced a claim to achieve better outcomes.

United Policyholders is a good resource you can point customers toward in order to better educate themselves. In their post **Top 10 Insurance Claim Tips** they state,

> *"Be proactive in the claim process and keep good notes. Make sure you maintain a paper trail. From the moment that you call your insurance company regarding a potential or active insurance claim, you should be taking detailed notes. Track names, dates, conversations, instructions, agreements, commitments, etc[23]."*

If everyone is committed to The Standard, there can be clarifying conversations that aid in arriving at an agreement on the scope and the cost of the project. Worksite conditions don't lie, but there can be some interpretation about what is and is not relevant to the claim at hand.

- If the adjuster does not agree with a scope item, they should be asking the contractor to clarify or further support the description as well as the strategy.
- If the customer does not agree with an objection from the carrier, they should ask for the adjuster to reference the policy language that would exclude the item from the claim.
- If the contractor does not agree with the settlement from the carrier, they will need to have an honest conversation with the customer about what they will and will not do for the cost that the customer is willing to commit to.

---

[22] ARES Restoration *Insurance Claims Questions* https://youtu.be/u6qVUDdoqUQ

[23] United Policyholders *Top 10 Insurance Claim Tips* https://uphelp.org/claim-guidance-publications/top-10-insurance-claim-tips/

The policy should cover the scope necessary to restore the property to resemble its pre-loss conditions. There can be some gray areas with regard to the scope and third-party objective support may be necessary to verify some conditions. The policy should cover the cost necessary to restore the property to resemble its pre-loss conditions. The cost is typically where there is a greater degree of discussion. We will continue to discuss some of the approaches to clearly communicating the story of the loss and supporting your pricing.

Accurate Data Input

Agreeing on the scope of work starts with agreeing on the source of the loss and identifying the extent of the damages. The data input, or estimating, process is how we translate the details we have captured into an invoice for mitigation services (often after the work is completed) or an estimate for reconstruction (usually before the work starts).

Your estimating process includes your estimating platform. How is the value of removal (mitigation) or replacement (repairs) best determined? You might be surprised to hear what insurance carrier State Farm declares on their own website:

> *"The most appropriate way to estimate the replacement cost of your home is to hire a building contractor or other building reconstruction professional to produce a detailed replacement cost estimate[24]."*

While many contractors would utter a hearty amen to these sentiments, these words also outline the high calling of the restoration contractor in the insurance claims process. The contractor's role is to provide the expertise and means to restore the damaged property to a pre-loss condition. To do so as a business they must be capable of doing so at a profit.

---

[24] State Farm *What is the difference between replacement cost and market value?*
https://www.statefarm.com/simple-insights/residence/replacement-cost-vs-market-value

Xactimate is one resource that can help to create a common language between the contractor and the carrier through standardized unit pricing. You may be reading this and thinking,

"What the heck is Xactimate?" Most professionals in property restoration are aware that this tool was developed by the Lovelands, who were contractors, as an estimating tool for insurance claims. Mark Whatley of Actionable Insights recalls in his article covering *The History and Future of Xactimate*:

> *"Starting in 1989, Xactware pioneered a scientific approach to providing building cost data for the restoration ecosystem. From the outset, Xactware's primary function has been to report market prices based upon industry surveys and recent transactions that have occurred[25]."*

Xactimate estimates are presented in a format that is different from most estimating structures within the skilled trades. Xactimate estimates are composed line by line, using standardized pricing. It should be recognized that insurance companies are seeking some semblance of predictability in claims. Averages are not inherently evil, but standardized prices should serve as a benchmark not the ceiling. **Xactware states**

> *"Since Xactware's published cost information is a reported market price based on recently acquired submissions, there is no way to be certain that any published price will be appropriate for a specific contractor, repair, or structure."*

In case you didn't catch that, Xactimate does not set your price. The estimating software is designed to be customized and adapted to real world costs in line with execution of The Standard.

> *"Having cost information that is based on recently submitted prices, however, is an extremely valuable tool in creating appropriate repair estimates, providing a basis from which the estimator can then decide whether the price should be accepted or adjusted[26]."*

[25] Whatley, M. (2018, April) *Xactimate: The History & The Future*. Actionable Insights. https://www.getinsights.org/resources/insighter-report/xact

When you create an accurate diagram (aka sketch) and compose your scope of work (laboriously) line by line and room by room, there are many helpful quantities that you can derive from this data within Xactimate. The software has many helpful tools but many contractors feel it has also been leveraged to cap what is owed to policyholders. Whatever program you utilize to draft your estimates, you need to understand how to appropriately charge for your total costs as you develop an agreed-upon scope of work.

If you cannot use a tool safely, you do not know how to do it right, and you should not be using it until you have proven otherwise. Improper use of a hand or power tool puts yourself and your team at risk. The same is true for estimating tools. While misuse of tools like Xactimate will not put your team members in immediate physical harm, it does lead to much frustration as it relates to being able to produce the work on budget and to the customers' satisfaction.

If you want to grow in this industry, you need to learn to master your tools and develop your ability to communicate effectively with all types of people. With regards to the use of estimating tools, Mark Cornelius, President of Emergency Mitigation Technician Academy (EMTA):

> *"Instead of worrying about how much you can charge for the hammer, learn how to use the hammer to its utmost capabilities. Become the most proficient person on the planet with that hammer. The money takes care of itself."*

If you are upset about a line item being rejected, are you certain that you used the right line item to reflect the scope that you are communicating? There are simple ways that you can set yourself apart and it all starts with learning to master the tools you are using. In many cases, it does not take much effort to stand out from the status quo. Start with a good framework, be consistent in how you gather and input data, and pay

[26]

https://eservice.xactware.com/esc/showme/PDF/2021/3312PricingMethodologySummary2a.pdf

attention to what gets questioned so that you can learn to better articulate your scope.

> ***Many estimators try <u>the spaghetti method</u> of throwing everything against the wall and hoping it sticks; this is not intentional estimating.***

Let's review the basic structure of how Xactimate is configured and uncover some of the areas where you can set yourself apart as an estimator.

Xactimate Structure

There are certain categories in Xactimate that are predictive, such as:

DRY = Drywall
PNT = Painting
FRM = Framing & rough carpentry

Other categories are a bit more obscure, such as:

CSF = Cleaning
FNC = Finish carpentry/trim work
EQU = Heavy equipment

Items such as flooring will become common abbreviations within your team if you understand the structure. Note, Floor Covering = FC, and then you add the type, for example:

FCW = Floor covering wood (which includes laminate)
FCV = Floor covering vinyl
FCC = Floor covering carpet

Even when you memorize the categories, structure, and location of common line items, you will still be utilizing the search bar as items are added, updated, or made obsolete. I have found that when you memorize these line items, you can write your scope notes or tick sheet in these codes during the site walk. For example, if I am going to do a drywall repair my notes may look like this:

Bedroom 1
DRY ½- 8x2
DRY PATCHJ 2+8+2
DRY TEX 12*4 (2' beyond repair)
DRY PNT P- 12*4 (PVA seal new wallboard prior to texture)
DRY PNT SP 16*6 (2' beyond texture)
DRY PNT P 24*8 (Paint affected wall corner to corner, one coat)

See the Four Estimating Approaches in Module 3

Another area where this is helpful is the difference between the LF (linear foot) of base cabinets, the SF (square foot) of laminate counters, and the LF of tile splash and edging. For example:

Kitchen
CAB LOW 12+5 LF (Island w/ 2 ELE)
LAM 14*2 + 7*3 (the counter has 2' for the dishwasher, and the island top extends 1' in all directions)
Note: Pay attention to the sheet sizes for laminate tops, for a 14' long top we may need two 8' sheets or one 16' sheet. Account for the waste in the laminate and the particle board substrate.
Wood Edge 14+2+2+7+7+3+3
Tile Splash 14+2
Note: Use the tile line item for the quantity of the splash, but don't forget to add the backsplash surcharge in XM8 as well as the caulking for the transition between the tile and the countertop.

It should be no surprise that communication is critical. In an estimate, scope notes are critical for communicating deviations from the "norms" as well as unique aspects of the project - whether those are related to the structure or the client preferences. If you are using Xactimate, F9 (or line item notes) are important to help you explain why a certain scope is necessary. A clear F9 note with a labeled photo can resolve many estimate questions or requests for revision with the carrier, the customer, as well as your production team.

A Defensible Estimate

Thorough Data Capture

+ Accurate Data Input

= Defensible Estimate

Estimating the Work (Phase 1)

Some restoration contractors have chosen to move away from Xactimate, either using another estimating platform or creating their own pricing. There are various estimating strategies and pricing structures. In my opinion, Xactimate is familiar to most insurance representatives, so it creates a shared language that can be utilized even if you customize your pricelist (recommended) or use time and materials (T&M) or lump sum pricing. On the other hand, some contend that using Xactimate only allows the adjuster to easily reject your line items and reduce your pricing.

I can tell you that when contractors reach out to me because an adjuster has asked them to present their estimate in Xactimate, I always tell them to get it in writing that the adjuster will pay the Xactimate pricing. Often the pricing from the contractor is lower than Xactimate. This is not to say that Xactimate pricing is spot on, but rather that many contractors, especially those just starting out, do not know how to properly price work to account for their overhead costs and their profitability goals.

I go over various estimating approaches in my prior book, unit or standardized pricing are examples and Xactimate is one of the estimating softwares available. As Bebo Crain says, "Before you learn any software, whichever program you use, learn how to fundamentally build your costs specific to your business activity, operation, and management." The basics of estimating are:

- Your direct costs (COGS) +
- Your indirect costs (overhead) +
- Your profit
- = Your sale price

It should be clearly understood that Xactware states in their Pricing Methodology Summary that their estimating program (Xactimate) is designed to be modified and customized.

> "Published price list is not intended to account for or provide costs for every potential item. Xactimate, therefore, provides users the full capability to create and/ or modify any costs as needed to match the conditions of the specific job or their company[27]."

In his capacity as the Advocacy and Government Affairs (AGA) Restoration Advocate, Ed Cross has worked alongside the pricing committee chair Ben Justesen, and many other volunteers, to produce the RIA position paper on deviation from standardized price lists. These position papers are designed to equip restoration contractors with consensus language from the industry that they can present when faced with hindrances to their ability to conduct business effectively.

> "The accurate or the right price is not something that is "global" in nature. Instead, it must be specific to the job. The right price is based upon the location, the accessibility, the conditions, the needs of the consumer or the customer, and the needs of the contractor with regards to overheads, target margins, and other factors[28]."

---

[27] *Pricing Methodology Summary*. Xactware.
https://eservice.xactware.com/esc/showme/PDF/2021/3312PricingMethodologySummary2a.pdf

While it is helpful to know what contractors of similar operating size and structure are doing, the right price is not based on what others are charging. Unit or standardized pricing can be excellent benchmarks for cost consistency, but they are not "industry standard". The RIA position paper continues,

> ***"Ultimately, the usual and customary cost of the work is determined between buyers and sellers in the marketplace.*** *Insurers that do not allow deviation from standardized prices are not using pricing software as it is intended and are at risk of not honoring their responsibilities under the contract of insurance."*

Carriers who do not recognize this customization afforded in tools such as Xactimate or Symbility are not utilizing the tool within its intended framework. In the aforementioned *Cross Examination* from Ed Cross, there are resources that the contractor can advise the policyholder to review if they feel their case needs to move in another direction.

Negotiating the Work (Phase 2)

The agreed-upon scope with the insurance company forms the basis for the contracted work, cost, and even the timeline for project completion. There are three key phases in the scoping process which we outline in The DYOJO Scoping Diagrams.

Each phase needs to be satisfied in order to proceed to the following. These phases include:

- Estimating
- Negotiating
- Producing

---

[28] Restoration Industry Association (RIA) Restoration Pricing Position Statement #1 https://www.restorationindustry.org/sites/default/files/docs/ria-pricing-position-statement-1-web.pdf

According to Merriam-Webster, **to negotiate** means to, "Obtain or bring about by discussion." Before we assume that a review or rejection by an insurance representative is an affront to our existence, we should take a step back and understand what they are asking. <u>Business is a negotiation</u>.

If you take the carrier out of the equation, you are often negotiating with your clients. Part of a successful negotiation is clearly defining the scope and expectations of the project so that you can accurately bid the cost of materials and labor. Yet, if the carrier is paying for the work, they have the right to ask whether the scope has been accurately presented and thoroughly supported. The second meaning for "negotiate" is to, "Find a way over or through (an obstacle or difficult path)."

You can view the adjuster as your adversary, but assuming so from the get-go only gives them one option - to be adversarial. Or you can proceed with the mindset to attempt to understand their position, in light of The Standard, and find a means to reach a mutually agreeable outcome. Treat professionals, even claims reviewers, as professionals who have a legitimate job to do, and see if you can't arrive at a better project outcome.

I had the pleasure of discussing the claims process with independent adjuster Peter Crosa at an event in January 2022. Peter shared some helpful insights for the claims negotiation process in **Cleanfax Magazine**, the conclusion of which he stated:

> *"Don't be dissuaded. Continue to explain your position and try to educate both the adjuster and property owner on the process and your reasoning. It will benefit the property owner and — ultimately — the insurance company[29]."*

After outlining three common adjuster mindsets and habits (which I encourage you to digest), he advised restorers:

> *"Be diplomatic and professional at all times. Your perceived disposition should be that you are concerned that the property damages are resolved correctly and that the insurance company's interests are protected as well."*

---

[29] Crosa, P. *The Art Of Negotiating With Adjusters*. Cleanfax Magazine. https://cleanfax.com/restoration/the-art-of-negotiating-with-adjusters/

Producing the Work (Phase 3)

Producing the work is still part of the scoping process as it is the execution of the effort in the prior phases. As an estimator, you MUST understand your role in relation to the processes that follow from an approved scope. Most projects have either change orders or supplements, which are contractual revisions to the agreed-upon scope. The estimator usually gets re-engaged when there are <u>alterations to the scope, cost, or duration</u> of the project so that they can assist the project managers to revise the contract.

Communication is key. The estimator has conversations with the adjuster and the customer. By the time the estimator has navigated all of these steps to produce an estimate, there are too many conversations and nuances to be able to recap effectively to the project manager. It's like a game of telephone. One way to offset the communication gap that inevitably happens with this system is to have whoever will be producing the work, and thereby the person who will be hands-on with the project the longest.

Whether you have an integrated business management system or not, you need to have a habit and means of regularly documenting the conversations with the carrier and the customer. Wherever you capture these interactions, it must be in a shared resource that is accessible by everyone who will be involved with the project. It's not enough to capture the worksite details and create a defensible estimate, the details of the scope must translate into an executable action plan for the production team.

To the estimator:

Recognize your role in and responsibility to the entire production process. You must communicate with the adjuster, the customer, and your production team if the project will be brought to a successful outcome. Chris Tilkov, the founder of Ask AiME, joined us for The DYOJO Podcast[30] and shared a few tips for aspiring professionals and growth-minded estimators, including:

Think in the broader context of your team. When you write an estimate you are representing "real people's work" and therefore it is essential to thoroughly capture what is needed to charge a fair price so that you can continue to pay a fair wage.

Think like an adjuster. As a member of the triangle of restoration, you are part of the process of accurately inputting a scope of work that represents what is needed to restore the structure to resemble pre-loss conditions with materials of like kind and quality (the standard).

To the owner/manager:

Spaghetti Estimators, as mentioned in this Module, are the product of an unclear, inconsistent, and unaccountable estimating system. Take the following steps to help develop and improve your process:

Develop a process to help you consistently capture thorough data relevant to the claim.

Create and/or refer to a database of carrier guidelines (most adjusting firms have these resources).

Internal review can help you to get ahead of rejections. Especially for larger or higher-end claims, have people in your network that you can utilize to get a second set of eyes on your estimate.

There are third party services, such as **Ask AiME**, that can provide you with an instant review and suggestions for items you may have missed and may also provide carrier profiles which help you identify common items specific to that organization.

To The Aspiring Professional

The structure of Xactimate and the shorthand I discussed can be helpful items to integrate into your documentation. You can

---

[30] The DYOJO Podcast Episode 69 - https://www.youtube.com/watch?v=MFDpM-RAorU

learn to integrate a common language with upstream team members. Several of the references in this Module, and throughout this book, will give you a roadmap to career growth. Be a student of the industry and you will elevate your ability to contribute to it.

Within your intentional estimating toolbag you now have:
- The Claims Standard
- A To-Scale Sketch and Numerous Labeled Photos
- A Simple Estimating Formula

Module 3 Quiz

1. What are the four phases of an insurance claims estimate?

2. It is as important to clarify what _____ _____ in the agreed-upon scope of work as it is to clarify what <u>is</u> in it. Why is that?

3. The contractor is primarily responsible for the scope of work as outlined in what document?

4. The adjuster is primarily responsible for the coverage of the claim as outlined in what document?

Additional Resources

Read **the article** *3 Key Ways to Elevate Your Estimating Process* in Construction Business Owner Magazine - https://www.constructionbusinessowner.com/estimating/3-key-ways-elevate-your-estimating-process

Watch **the video** *Using Questions During Business Negotiations* from The DYOJO Podcast - https://www.youtube.com/watch?v=_YExoRy0Wmg&t=58s

Read **the article** *The Art and Science of Insurance Claims Estimating* in C&R Magazine - https://candrmagazine.com/the-art-and-science-of-insurance-claims-estimating/

The DYOJO Scoping Diagram, Pt. 2

PRODUCING

TheDYOJO.com/scope

NEGOTIATING

SCOPE

ESTIMATING

PHASE 3 - Producing
Executing the agreed-upon scope
- Client Communication
- Carrier Communication
- Production Communication

PHASE 2: Negotiating
Composing the agreed-upon scope
- Client Communication - Clear and Consistent
- Carrier Communication - Early and Often

PHASE 1 - Estimating
Establishing the agreed-upon scope
- Data Capture - Thorough
- Data Input - Accurate

Module Four

Preparing To Be Profitable

<u>A well written estimate does not guarantee a successful project, but a poorly written estimate is a terrible way to start one.</u> A lackluster estimate stemming from an insufficient scope will result in complications leading to:

- Production frustration
- Lack of efficiency
- Unhappy customers
- Inconsistent outcomes
- Lower profitability

If you regularly experience the five items above, you will want to STOP what you are currently doing and determine what you can START[31] doing to improve your performance. We often focus on the financial outcomes, but these should be data points that open our perspectives to broader issues within our estimating and production processes. As a person in a position of leadership, you are responsible for clarifying your organization's unique and consistently followed **process** for everything, including estimating.

We distinguish the *Process* (internal) from *Production* (external) in *the Four Pillars of Success*[32]. If you want to have consistent project outcomes (external) you need to be clear and consistent with your internal processes. The agreed-upon scope should be based upon thorough data capture and accurate data input. The production process should start with thorough data transfer and accurate production planning.

---

[31] Read more on Start - Stop from Lex Sisney - https://organizationalphysics.com/2019/09/18/communicating-for-better-faster-change-management/

[32] thedyojo.com/pillars

Everyone has to play their part in starting off on the right track and keeping things moving in the right direction.

My pursuit of restoration history reached a recent high point when I had the pleasure of co-authoring an article with Pete Consigli for Cleanfax. Our article was titled ***Building A Bridge***[33] *From Restoration's Founding Fathers To The Modern Restorer.* There is <u>so much</u> that restorers-present can and should learn from not-so-long-ago restoration past.

Throughout his career, Pete trained restorers to value **the Restoration Triangle.** Each party brings something unique to the table that should be heard and referenced as the agreed-upon scope is established:

> **The insured** (who's damaged) has a unique perspective on the pre-loss conditions and the extent of the loss.
>
> **The carrier** representative (who's payin' for it) has a unique perspective regarding the details of the policy and the responsibility of the carrier with regards to the source and extent of damages—as well as any relevant exclusions.
>
> **The contractor** (who's fixin' it) has a unique perspective on the means, methods, and material costs that will be relevant to establishing an agreed-upon scope of work to restore the structure.

Pete reminds stakeholders:

> *"If one of these parties is left out of the process of determining and agreeing on the extent of damage, scope of repair, cost of restoration to a pre-loss condition, timelines, and criteria for satisfactory completion, then there will be problems."*

A claim should not follow the narrative of a T.V. drama or the strategy for *Survivor*, whereby two members of the triangle team

---

[33] Consigli, P. & Isaacson, J. (2022 January) *Building A Bridge From Restoration's Founding Fathers To The Modern Restorer.* Cleanfax. https://cleanfax.com/management/restoration-industrys-history/

up to push their narrative through. For example, the contractor and client should not be in cahoots to figure out a way to "maximize the claim" without justification. This is fraud. Neither should the contractor and the carrier be working together to dwindle the scope. This is short-changing (and likely grounds for bad faith).

The carrier should not be able to deny a scope item "just because" (arbitrarily) nor should the contractor expect that a scope item is approved "just because" (also arbitrary).

Ed Cross, The Restoration Lawyer, reminds all parties of the responsibility of the insurance policy as a contract between the policyholder and the policy provider. Carriers and their representatives, "Are prohibited from making arbitrary claims handling decisions." As we have said they are bound by the policy and that does not include finding the cheapest price possible or holding contractors to standardized pricing. Ed says

in his *Cross Examination* column,

"One of the Ten Commandments of insurance claims handling law is "Thou shalt not misrepresent coverage," but some of them are doing it routinely. If they say "we don't pay for that," they need an objectively reasonable justification, or they face liability for insurance bad faith[34]."

Setting yourself up for success in the restoration process requires identifying the extent and degree of damages. The insured should expect that their damaged property will be physically inspected by at least one competent person during this determination. Upon completion of a site inspection, a scope of work must be prepared and agreed upon. The RIA Code of Ethics calls upon restorers to:

---

[34] Cross, E (2022, April 14) *Cross Examination: Who Is In Charge Of Setting Restoration Prices?* R&R Magazine.
https://www.randrmagonline.com/articles/90063-cross-examination-who-is-in-charge-of-setting-restoration-prices

"Provide our customers with accurate information concerning the scope of work required and its costs, maintaining strict impartiality in our professional opinions."

Adjusters and contractors should be able to communicate so that laymen can understand the why of their approach to observed damages. Even estimate reviewers are capable of asking good questions. It is incumbent upon both parties to complete thorough data capture of the conditions of the damaged structure. Pete reminds all parties:

"Damage assessment is a complex process that entails training and experience. It is important that the experts provide an explanation for their recommendations to either do or not to do something."

You don't have to agree to everything, but you should be aware of how certain carriers prefer the claim to be presented. <u>Understand who you are communicating with:</u>

An adjuster and/or claims reviewer who likely will never step foot on the job site

A customer who doesn't understand the claims process Set the expectations at the first meeting, and educate your customer. Follow up your communication with emails to document discussions and ensure the information has a better chance of getting through. Educate your customer about the estimate scoping, writing, submitting, and review process. One of the best things that you can do is keep your customer informed about every step of the process.

The Restoration Triangle

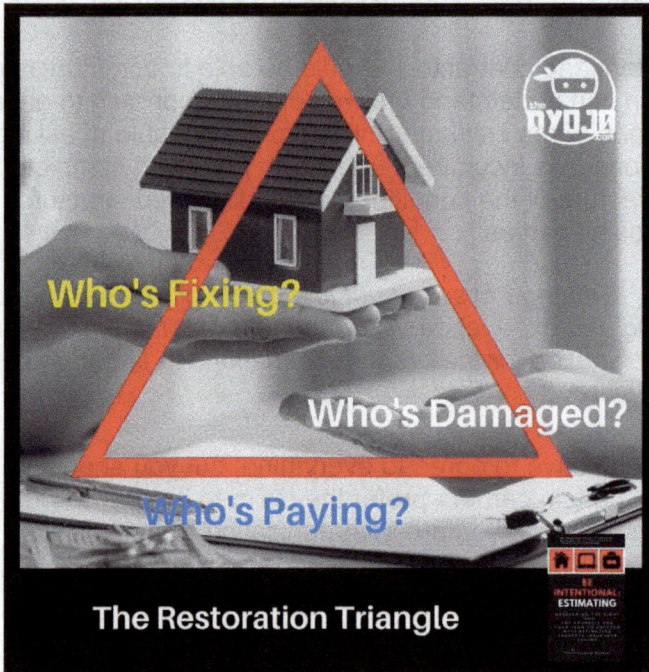

Restorers complain that adjusters rebuff their estimates or invoices. It's their job, to adjust, which at minimum would be to review for accuracy. If you are committed to thorough data capture and accurate data input, a request for clarification should not be an affront to your dignity as a restorer. If you have not supported the scope or cost of something, you either need to explain it better or revise it.

Many would call this making concessions, in my mind, concessions are only those legitimate scope items that a party, such as a customer or the carrier, is requesting a change unrelated to a lack of evidence.

Concession **is simply defined as a thing that is granted, especially in response to demands; the act of yielding something.**

The question is not whether we make concessions in business, but whether we yield to legitimate requests based on a lack of supporting documentation or from pragmatism. As a matter of practice, the restorer should be working for the customer. As professionals with experience in claims processing, we should, with the customer's consent and inclusion, be communicating regularly with the carrier.

How do you gain ground on the claims review process? Here are some suggestions to start tracking data to inform decisions and find a resolution:

Do you review your rejections for trends? You can do this as a team or you can do this as an individual estimator. You can download the PDF for The DYOJO *Tracking Claims Review Worksheet* or you can develop your own system.

Change your mindset. If we change our mindset from "winning and losing" with an opponent to determining whether a request is <u>founded</u> (reasonable review queries based upon the standards, practices, and carrier guidelines), <u>unfounded</u> (contradictory to standards, practices, and carrier guidelines), or <u>in the gray area</u> (subject to interpretation). If you download our worksheet you will notice these are the categories.

Change your process. The status quo is to complain about the system. If you are approaching your profession with a growth mindset you will work to find solutions to your issues. Start by tracking your rejections so that you can make decisions based upon objective data rather than your collective-subjective opinions.

You should be keeping detailed records of all of your communication, including following up every conversation with an email and advising your customers to do the same. A key part of the documentation is getting **everything in writing**[35]. If your team members do not consistently capture data and your estimators do not effectively communicate the story of the loss, is that a failure of the tools (i.e. Xactimate) or the fault of the carrier (or vendor programs)?

---

[35] Insurance Claim Tip #1 - Keep Notes of Everything - https://www.youtube.com/watch?v=HkFPGQcgMA8

If you keep playing or allow the same poorly executed estimating games you shouldn't be surprised when you get the same poor results. As an owner, manager, and estimator, you are responsible to develop and improve the estimating process. Former Navy Seal, Jocko Wilinik, has an excellent quote:

"When setting expectations, no matter what has been said or written, if substandard performance is accepted and no one is held accountable—if there are no consequences—that poor performance becomes the new standard. Therefore, leaders must enforce standards."

In our industry, the standards of care serve as the baseline consensus best practices by which restoration contractors should perform their functions. If you follow the standards of

care, you are setting the foundation for *Doing It Right* but you should not rest your efforts at this level. Standards of care should not be confused with the highest, best, and/or innovative actions that a contractor could take. In his book **Leadership in Restorative Drying**[36], Ken Larsen, shares three important distinctions for our industry:

Standard Practice is a phrase used to describe practices normally and regularly performed by professionals of a trade. They may or may not reflect competence.

Standard of Care in the structural restorative drying industry has been defined [by the IICRC S500 consensus body standard committee] to be: "practices that are common to reasonably prudent members of the trade who are recognized in the industry as qualified and competent."

State of the Art refers to the highest level of general development, as of a device, technique or scientific field achieved at a particular time.

These distinctions apply to estimating best practices as well, which your team should develop internally. Estimators should be

---

[36] Leadership in Restorative Drying by Ken Larsen - https://www.amazon.com/Leadership-Restorative-Drying-Csds-Larsen/dp/1457529017

as acquainted with the standards of care as the front line employees. Estimators, managers, and owners should be pushing themselves to learn and incorporate best practices into every aspect of the organization (*Do It Excellently*).

Just because you have written "thousands of estimates" does not mean that you don't still have things to learn regarding the scope of work and effectively composing estimates. Mike McGuinness gave a presentation for AEML Winter Break 2022[37] on what restorers and assessors can learn from dumb things he has observed (over many years) as a building scientist. He quoted Hall of Fame Green Bay Packers football coach, and the man for whom the Superbowl trophy is now named, Vince Lombardi[38] who is credited with saying, ***"Practice does not make perfect. Only perfect practice makes perfect."***

Being open to constructive criticism and continually seeking ways to improve in your craft is going to help propel you towards being the best that you can be. As an estimator, it is helpful to have field experience in the types of work that you will be writing scopes for. I encourage all owners and managers to promote from within and to cross-train. When you've observed the work or performed it, you have a fuller understanding of the production requirements which in turn better informs your pricing strategy.

Everyone should remember that it is their job to make the next person's job easier (to the extent possible). This is why some element of cross-training among teams and responsibilities is helpful to the mindset and habits of your team members. For example, if your demolition crew understands what your drywall team has to do in order to repair flood cuts, they might take that extra time to pull nails and make straight cuts in the drywall during removal.

No one is more important than the other members of the team. Each role and responsibility should be respected by the others.

---

[37] For more on the AEML Winter Break 2022, read this Cleanfax interview with Pete Consigli - https://cleanfax.com/news/aeml-winter-break-2022/

[38] Chapter 1 of my project management book builds on a quote from Lombardi regarding "the will to prepare to win."

If the estimators are untouchable and unaccountable, your team members aren't going to care about making their job easier - likely the opposite. When a team member is "untouchable" the other members of the team will create a game out of making that person's job harder.

The Three R's

Previously we introduced the Three D's (documentation). You want to create a clear expectation that documentation is not optional. Everyone must document everything and the people in a position of leadership should be leading by example in this area. Now we will discuss *the Three R's* that will help you prepare for and be successful in the world of insurance claims estimating. These are not required, but they will surely help you if you are willing to learn from:

> **Rejection**
> **Repetition**
> **Relationships**

Learning from rejection

I believe that a key mindset in business, especially sales, is to make people say no to your face. If I am in a room full of people and I want to sell them this mediocre book, I might be scared to approach them because they could say no. The truth is, unless people are flooding (intentional pun) to meet me, they are already saying no to me. They just haven't done it to my face.

I always share this with new salespeople, the customer has already been saying no to us, so don't let that be a barrier. You have nothing to lose other than your false sense of pride. If you aren't willing to risk an awkward conversation, then you may feel good about yourself but you have not achieved your goal of introducing yourself and advancing towards the prospect of a sale.

Rejection is a part of life and it is a part of the business. Not

everyone is going to say "yes" to you AND you should not say "yes" to every client or opportunity that comes your way. The best time to fire a bad client is before the job even starts. As it relates to being an estimator, if you don't do well with rejection, you're going to need to learn. There aren't many professions where dealing with some form of rejection is key to being able to achieve your goals. For insurance claims estimating, rejection can come from many sources. We cover the types of people you will interact with, during the claims process, in my first book.

If you submit an estimate to insurance, you can be subject to any combination of persons who are representatives of the insurance carrier. They all have opinions and are eager to resolve the issues with your estimate that affect their position. There is a difference between a rejection and a review request. **The contractor can always decide HOW they will respond.** Even if the carrier representative is being demanding, often the best response is in the form of a question. As Steven Patrick, of Level the Playing Field, shared on **our podcast**[39], ask the adjuster, "Please tell me why you feel that way," or start your conversation with, "Could you please help me understand…"

Learning from repetition

As previously mentioned, you should start your claims investigation and scope by answering two questions, WHERE did this loss start (source) and WHAT did it affect (extent)? You can choose whether you start in the affected room or the area furthest from the damages. Your approach to inspecting and documenting the site conditions should always be the same in that you start from the top-down.

This same top-down approach to documenting the site conditions will carry over to the framework for our estimate. I believe **headers** are a good way to separate out your scope items both to ensure you capture everything (internal) as well as communicate in a more effective and orderly fashion with the estimate reviewers (external).

---

[39] The DYOJO Podcast Episode 79 - https://www.youtube.com/watch?v=GCIINvj5vZc

#	Cat	Sel	Act	Notes	Description	Coverage
				▯	.	
				▯	PREP ITEMS:	
				▯	.	
				▯	WALLS & CEILINGS:	
				▯	.	
				▯	TRIM & PAINT:	
				▯	.	
				▯	FLOORS & CLEANING:	

My most frequent headers include:
- Prep Items
- Walls & Ceilings
- Trim & Paint
- Floors & Cleaning

You can get as detailed as you want by having those core categories capitalized and in bold with sub-categories only in bold. For example, a basic header structure in a room might include:

ROOM: _____

PREP ITEMS:
- Masking
- Contents
- Additional demolition
- Detach and reset items

WALLS & CEILINGS:
- Wall and/or ceiling repairs
- If there is significant cabinet work you might make a sub-header

TRIM & PAINT:
- Baseboard, casing, and/or moulding
- Prime and paint

FLOORS & CLEANING:
- Flooring repairs

- Cleaning specific items and openings
- Final cleaning

MITIGATION
- Mitigation headings would include prep items, equipment, removal, and monitoring.

TIME & MATERIALS
- Even if you use time and materials for your estimate, you can segment your billing recap by room or area into category headings for a much cleaner and easier-to-follow estimate. Oftentimes, for larger mitigation projects, I would break out our scope of work with a header for each day or week.

The goal is to tell the story. Repetition helps ensure you don't miss items either in the data capture (scoping) or the data input (estimating) phases. Help your clients follow your approach to the loss and set your estimates apart from the status quo. Using the framework from above creates a key to the "map" so that they, and the claims representatives, can follow the scope of work.

Learning from relationships

My friend David Smith says, "Know your audience and situation. Not every loss or person you work with is the same, so why would your estimates be? Great estimators have the ability to understand their audience and tell a story through their details to reach that audience." You have to deal with rejection, but as a professional, you should also be continually building professional relationships with everyone that you work with:

Internal relationships with all staff including frontline employees, production staff, and administrative team members

External relationships with adjusters, vendors, and clients

As a general rule, seek ways to connect, collaborate, and conquer. Whenever there is a conflict, try to determine what the shared objectives and values are and build from those common points rather than exacerbate whatever is driving you away from being able to accomplish your goals.

Many have commented that people do business with people that they know, like, and trust. I think this sequence is a bit out of order. If you want to do business, potential clients need to know you exist; no one can hire you if they don't even know

that you are an option. I believe in most cases, you have to build trust before people will like you.

In order to get an opportunity to prove this, you need to build rapport with local referral partners including agents, adjusters, property managers, etc. Once you have made them aware that you exist and you get your shot to prove that you are trustworthy, you need to make sure that you give them no reason not to trust you. Consumers and carriers should be able to trust that your scopes are accurate and backed by thorough documentation.

Within your intentional estimating toolbag you now have:
- The Claims Standard
- A To-Scale Sketch and Numerous Labeled Photos
- A Simple Estimating Formula
- The Restoration Triangle

Module 4 Questions
1.   What are the three types of standards?

        Standard P_____
        Standard of C_____
        State of the A_____

2.   Who are the three parties in the Restoration Triangle?

3.   Where do you go in Xactimate to discover what is and is not included in a line item?

4.   How helpful do you think formatting elements such as headers, top-down structure, and F9 notes are to the negotiation as well as the production phase of a project lifecycle?

Additional Resources

Watch **this video** on *Tripping Over Nickels While Leaving Behind Thousands Of Dollars* - https://www.youtube.com/watch?v=JzTMf2S8A-c&t=23s

Check out Ed Cross' *The Book on Restoration Collections* - https://edcross.com/restoration-collections-book/

For more information on estimate structure read **this article** on *The Format For Successful Fire Damage Restoration Estimates* - https://www.randrmagonline.com/articles/89290-the-format-for-successful-fire-damage-restoration-estimates

Check out the **AGA Position Papers** available to members of the RIA - https://www.restorationindustry.org/member-only-aga-resources

Richard Alexis(creator of the Indoor Environmental Science Forum), Cliff Zlotnik, Peter Crosa, and The AEML Winter Break pit crew Zeke Isaacson (taking a picture of me taking a picture) with Pete Consigli and IAQ Josh Winton in the background (on-screen). January 2022

Module Five

Leveling Up As An Estimator

We have addressed various levels of mindset and habits for better project outcomes, let's apply some of what we have been discussing to a scenario. For this example, we will be discussing four common estimating approaches to drywall repairs. Please note, that what I am about to share is basic and is not intended to be a prescription to cure your ailments. These examples show some of the potential pickups that can be gained by the contractor, simply by taking their time learning to operate their estimating tool.

The scope:

Our affected wall is twelve feet (12') wide by eight feet (8') high.

The area of repair is 8' wide by 2' high (an 8 LF flood cut).

A Common SF Estimate

If you are new to Xactimate, you may think this is a good way to write an estimate. It seems sensible enough, right? Take the

square footage (SF) of the affected wallboard, apply the same to the seal and paint and then paint the whole affected wall corner to corner. You may have accounted for the basic scope but you will not have accounted for the lost productivity associated with a smaller scope of work. At scale, Xactimate pricing provides better margins for a contractor, i.e. the larger the project the more room there <u>should</u> be for profitability.

#	Cat	Sel	Act	Notes	Description	Coverage	Calc	Quantity	Unit
1	DRY	1/2+	+	🗒	1/2" drywall - hung, taped, heavy texture, read	Dwelling	8*2	16	SF
3	PNT	SP	+	🗒	Seal/prime then paint the surface area (2 coat	Dwelling	8*2	16	SF
5	PNT	P	+	🗒	Paint the surface area - one coat	Dwelling	12*8	96	SF

The Line Items Include:
- DRY ½+ = ½" drywall - hung, taped, heavy texture, ready for paint at 8' long by 2' high (16SF)
- PNT SP = Seal/prime then paint the surface area (2 coats) at the same 16SF as the wallboard repair
- PNT P = Paint the surface area - one coat for the whole wall (corner to corner) 12' x 8' (96SF)

While everyone wants to speak poorly about Xactimate, you will see in the following examples that you can't blame the estimating software if you are not using the tool correctly. For the price list at the time of this estimate, **the cost of this scope came out to $147.20**.

If this were the only room in your scope, there should be labor minimums that are initiated to help increase the total cost of the estimate. The economies of scale, by nature, are more difficult to achieve for smaller projects so it's important to be aware of methods to protect your ability to be profitable.

Common LF Estimate

As you use the program and begin to learn about the various line items, you notice that there is a linear foot (LF) line item for drywall that is designed to help close the gap in productivity lost when repairing a "flood cut". Typically a flood cut is a 2-foot (2') high cut in an affected length of wallboard, but they can be anywhere from 6 inches (6") to four feet (4'). By utilizing a more appropriate line item for the scope of work you will bring the estimated price of the work closer into sync with the scope and actual cost of the work.

#	Cat	Sel	Act	Notes	Description	Coverage	Calc	Quantity	Unit
6	DRY	LF	+	🗂	1/2" - drywall per LF - up to 2' tall	Dwelling	8	8	LF
26	DRY	TEX	+	🗂	Texture drywall - light hand texture	Dwelling	8*2	16	SF
7	PNT	SP	+	🗂	Seal/prime then paint the surface area (2 coat	Dwelling	8*2	16	SF
8	PNT	P	+	🗂	Paint the surface area - one coat	Dwelling	12*8	96	SF

The Line Items Include:
- DRY LF = ½" - drywall per LF - up to 2' tall (8LF)

- DRY TEX = Texture drywall - light hand texture 8' x 2' (16SF) at the same 16SF as the wallboard repair
- PNT SP = Seal/prime then paint the surface area (2 coats) at the same 16SF as the texture repair
- PNT P = Paint the surface area - one coat for the whole wall (corner to corner) 12' x 8' (96SF)

This basically shows the variance between 16SF with DRY ½+ and 8LF with DRY LF. **The cost of this scope is $202.08**. If this were the only room in your scope, there should be labor minimums that are initiated to help increase the total cost of the estimate.

Common Program Compliant Estimate

When I say "program compliant", I mean an estimate structure that is least likely to meet resistance by common estimate review platforms. I have worked in program or a third-party administrator (TPA) work for the majority of my career.
While we work to keep this revenue generation source at a specific percentage of our overall work, there are many challenges to this system that contractors are not fond of.

#	Cat	Sel	Act	Notes	Description	Coverage	Calc	Quantity	Unit
21	DRY	1/2-	+	🗂	1/2" drywall - hung, taped, ready for texture	Dwelling	8*2	16	SF
22	DRY	PATCHJ	+	🗂	Tape joint for new to existing drywall - per LF	Dwelling	2+8+2	12	LF
23	DRY	TEX	+	🗂	Texture drywall - light hand texture	Dwelling	10*3	30	SF
24	PNT	SP	+	🗂	Seal/prime then paint the surface area (2 coat	Dwelling	10*3	30	SF
25	PNT	P	+	🗂	Paint the surface area - one coat	Dwelling	12*8	96	SF

<u>The Line Items Include:</u>
- DRY ½- = ½" drywall - hung, taped, ready for texture at 8' long by 2' high (16SF)
- DRY PATCHJ = Tape joint for new to existing drywall - per LF at 2' up + 8' long + 2' down (12LF)
- DRY TEX = Texture drywall - light hand texture at 1' beyond the repair on all sides so 10' long (1' beyond all sides) by 3' high (30SF)
- PNT SP = Seal/prime then paint the surface area (2 coats) at the same 30SF as the texture application
- PNT P = Paint the surface area - one coat for the whole wall (corner to corner) 12' x 8' (96SF)

Restoration contractors enjoy slinging verbal barbs against their peers who participate in program or TPA (third party administrator) work. As you can see, this is an example of a typical program "approved" estimate and it is significantly higher than the common SF and LF estimates that we often see.

If you cannot drive a screw properly, is that the fault of the impact driver? Learn to use the tools before you complain about how terrible they are. **The cost of this scope is $301.16.**

Common Non-program Estimate

As we have mentioned, just because there is a line item does not mean that it should be assumed it is correct or will be approved by anyone reviewing the estimate. If you have chosen to steer clear of program work, your estimate is still going to be reviewed by someone. At a minimum, your customer will review your estimate as will a representative from the insurance company, as discussed previously in the segment on The Restoration Triangle.

#	Cat	Sel	Act	Notes	Description	Coverage	Calc	Quantity	Unit
14	DRY	1/2-	I	▢	1/2" drywall - hung, taped, ready for texture -	Dwelling	8*2	16	SF
15	DRY	1/2-	M	▢	1/2" drywall - hung, taped, ready for texture -	Dwelling	32	32	SF
16	DRY	PATCHJ	+	▢	Tape joint for new to existing drywall - per LF	Dwelling	2+8+2	12	LF
18	PNT	S-	+	▢1	Seal the surface area w/PVA primer - one coat	Dwelling	10*3	30	SF
17	DRY	TEX	+	▢	Texture drywall - light hand texture	Dwelling	10*3	30	SF
19	PNT	SP	+	▢	Seal/prime then paint the surface area (2 coat	Dwelling	10*3	30	SF
20	PNT	P	+	▢	Paint the surface area - one coat	Dwelling	12*8	96	SF

The Line Items Include:
- DRY ½- (install only) = ½" drywall - hung, taped, ready for texture at 8' long by 2' high (16SF)
- DRY ½- (material only) = ½" drywall - hung, taped, ready for texture at a full sheet (32SF) as this is the material minimum. It should be noted that this scenario assumes we are only working in this one room, where there are multiple rooms "economies of scale" come into play that makes the standardized pricing work
- DRY PATCHJ = Tape joint for new to existing drywall - per LF at 2' up + 8' long + 2' down (12LF)
- DRY TEX = Texture drywall - light hand texture at 1' beyond the repair on all sides so 10' long by 3' high (30SF)

- PNT SP = Seal/prime then paint the surface area (2 coats) at the same 30SF as the texture application
- PNT P = Paint the surface area - one coat for the whole wall (corner to corner) 12' x 8' (96SF)

We are accounting for the waste in the drywall as we will purchase a full sheet (32 SF) but only be using half (16 SF).

Some would argue that you keep it and take it to the next job but that isn't always the case. We also added PVA primer as a typical job sequence prior to applying texture. **The cost of this scope is $332.68.**

Group	Subtotal	# Items
DRYWALL		
Common SF	$147.20	3
Common LF	$202.08	4
Program	$301.16	5
Program Rev	$324.52	5
Non Program	$332.68	7

Our Four Common Estimating Approaches result in the following totals:
Common SF estimate = $147.20
Common LF estimate = $202.08
Common Program estimate = $301.16
Common Non Program estimate = $332.68

Additional items relevant to this limited scope of work might include:

- Masking and dust control
- Removal of wallboard to studs/joists or 1x4 blocking for support of new materials
- Skim coat repaired surfaces prior to texture
- Detach and reset outlets with the installation of new wallboard
- Additional labor for any specialty items

While these examples don't cover every issue related to short scope or underutilization of line items, it paints a helpful picture of how sharpening your tools can help you initiate a better project outcome at the estimating phase. The moral of the story is to learn to utilize your tools properly before you blame them for your issues.

Simple Pricing Customizations

The final example was the "non-program estimate" which included a line item customization for material waste of the drywall and production sequence for PVA primer. These items may not fly in a program scenario, but there are some additional customizations that *should* be agreeable, even in the most stringent of circumstances.

SHOULD. Nothing is 100%. Just because this book says so, the course you took says so, or some keyboard warrior claims, "I don't negotiate with terrorists," does not mean that you can get every line item you want to be approved in every situation.

The Restoration Lawyer, Ed Cross, reminds us of the legal term "arbitrary and capricious," which goes for all parties of the Restoration Triangle if we are following The Standard. As such, a carrier representative should not be able to deny a scope item just because they say so, but neither should a contractor be able to demand one for the same faulty reason.

Arbitrary, according to Oxford, is, *"Based on random choice or personal whim, rather than any reason or system."* Many things in the insurance process, especially those in preferred vendor work, can feel random but they are actually elements of an agreement between the contractor and the referring organization. If you are an estimator, you may not have been in on the conversation when certain agreements were made, but it is to your benefit to learn the terms.

For the Common Program Compliant Estimate from above, **the cost of the scope was $301.16.**

We will compare this with a <u>Common Program Compliant Estimate Revised</u> with Simple Pricing Customizations.

We are going to make one simple change and then one more involved pricing customization. First, we will confirm the real-world materials cost for drywall, and then we will adjust the labor yield to account for the loss of productivity.

Drywall Materials - Components

To discover the material cost for the drywall we want to access the "Components" tab within Xactimate.

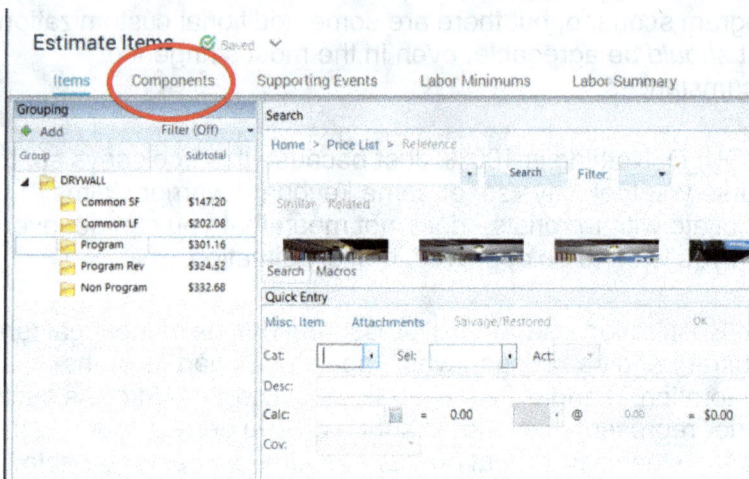

For our Common Program Estimate (from the prior chapter), the components are as follows:

Components List

Code	Description	Tax Status	Contractor Supplied	Quantity	Unit	Unit Price	Total
∧ Materials $33.69							
DRY1/2	Gypsum board, 1/2"	Taxable	Yes	18.93	SF	$0.460	8.71
DRYCBEAD	Metal corner bead	Taxable	Yes	0.89	LF	$0.345	0.31
DRYMUD	Drywall joint compound - 50 lb	Taxable	Yes	0.50	BX	$11.979	5.96*
DRYN	Drywall nails (based on 25 to 5	Taxable	Yes	0.04	LB	$1.766	0.07
DRYSCREW	Drywall screws - grabber - (ba	Taxable	Yes	0.08	LB	$2.730	0.23*
DRYTAPE	Joint tape - 500' roll	Taxable	Yes	0.04	RL	$6.016	0.22*
PNTL	Latex paint	Taxable	Yes	0.38	GL	$41.942	16.10*
PNTPUT	Painter's putty	Taxable	Yes	0.01	GL	$21.067	0.24*
PNTSANDP	160 - 180 grit sandpaper - per	Taxable	Yes	0.17	SH	$0.687	0.12
PNTSEALPVA	PVA - latex drywall primer/seal	Taxable	Yes	0.09	GL	$19.240	1.73
							$33.69

It may be difficult to see, but the first line in this Components list shows DRY ½ - Gypsum board, ½" is factored at $0.46/SF. We had factored 18.93SF of material (combined) so our budget is $8.71. I wanted to confirm this unit pricing was accurate so I pulled up the website for my local hardware store; for this example, we will use Lowes.

ToughRock

1/2-in 4-ft x 8-ft Mold-Guard Mold Resistant Moisture Resistant Regular Drywall Panel

Model #NA

$17.48   ★★★★☆ 196

🎁 **Free Store & Curbside Pickup**
288 Available today at Puyallup Lowe's

🚚 **Delivery** ⓘ
Scheduling Available on orders $50+

If the current, in-stock, ½" sheet of drywall at this store is $17.48 per unit. This would mean our square footage price is $17.48 divided by 32 SF which totals $0.546/SF (round up to $0.55). This is a variance of $0.09/SF which may not sound like

much, but multiply that delta over the course of the whole project times all of the projects that you do in a year that include drywall and now we are talking some serious money. Those small but legitimate pickups are margin points, and rather than profiting, you aren't even covering costs; you are going into a deficit.

You may be tempted to blame Xactimate, but it's a tool that updates at least monthly, taking the averages of the information that it receives on pricing. If you didn't read it here, would you have known to look for it? Anthony Nelson, whom we quoted in the preface, has been called *the- righter-of-material-cost-variance-wrongs* as he has collected data for his unique market on the pricing gaps between Xactimate and the local supply stores. If you aren't tracking it, how can you correct it?

Components List

Code	Description	Tax Status	Contractor Supplied	Quantity	Unit	Unit Price	Total
⌃ Materials	$35.29						
DRY1/2	Gypsum board, 1/2"	Taxable	Yes	18.76	SF	$0.550	10.32
DRYCBEAD	Metal corner bead	Taxable	Yes	0.88	LF	$0.345	0.30

In Components, I revised the price for drywall from $0.46/SF to $0.55/SF. This brought our materials base budget up from $8.71, not enough to buy a full sheet of ½" drywall at current market pricing, to $10.32.

This is closer to my real-world costs but still leaves us eating the variance for the waste. Refer to our Non-Program Estimate from above as one way to present this material minimum and bridge that gap.

With both of these fairly simple revisions, the Program Compliant Estimate Revised **increases from $301.16 to $324.52.** You may be tempted to complain that you shouldn't have to do this, and maybe you are right. But, most of the alternatives I have observed operate similarly if they update their pricing in real-time at all.

For each of these estimating scenarios, we have not accounted for some key pickups which might include:

- General Conditions - disposal of debris, cartage/travel, additional labor considerations, supervisory labor[40], etc.
- Prep Items - dust control barriers, surface protection, etc.
- Walls & Ceilings - various finishes, multiple paint colors, detach and reset outlets, outlet covers, etc.
- Trim & Paint - baseboard, casing, etc.
- Final cleaning
- Additional items might include - contents, insulation, carpet cleaning, etc.

Pricing Research Methodology

A software company does not set the prices for what a willing buyer will pay a willing contractor (aka a fair market cost). If you are using Xactimate in your business, it is to your advantage to learn all that you can about how the program is designed and how best to utilize that functionality to communicate your scope and cost. Thankfully, Xactware has been consistent in its effort to address questions and concerns about its platform. According to Xactware's *Pricing Research Methodology* paper updated February 6, 2018, their pricing is open for inspection.

"Xactware understands that job size and complexity have a dramatic effect on the costs associated with performing the work. It is important to note that when publishing a database that uses "installed unit prices," the prices must be based upon an assumption of job size and complexity[41]."

This is no surprise to the contractor, that the job size and complexity of the project play a role in the scope and cost. Restoration contractors will recognize that somehow this word

---

[40] Read more and watch a short video about supervisory labor - https://www.thedyojo.com/blog/supervisory-labor-direct-or-indirect-cost-for-contractors

[41] *Pricing Research Methodology* (2018, Feb 6) Xactware. https://www.xactware.com/globalassets/us/pdf/brochures/pricing-research-methodology.pdf

"complexity" has been weaponized to restrict items such as overhead and profit on claims. In a recent discussion with Steven Patrick, he remarked that this argument is moot given that the insurance process makes the project inherently more complex than it would be if the transaction were directly between the buyer and the seller.

Standardized pricing is not evil, nor is the effort by the carriers to have some predictability in pricing. Xactimate is designed for common scenarios, using standardized pricing, and I would argue, opening a common language for discussion of scope and cost. Yet, it has its flaws and limits. As Xactware outlines in this paper, you can inspect all of the components that go into a line item including materials, labor, definitions, and supporting events.

> *"Xactware's goal is to target the most common job scenario. However, understanding that prices can vary from job to job, Xactware has made every effort to ensure that all details associated with published prices are "Open for Inspection.""*

Let's take a look at this from our drywall scenario and zoom in on the labor yield in particular.

Drywall - Labor Yield

In the Quick Entry field, if you highlight the line item for DRY ½- and click on the price, the program will open a side screen to the right. The current setting shows a price of $2.48 per square foot (SF). So our 16SF at $2.48/SF nets a line item total of $39.68.

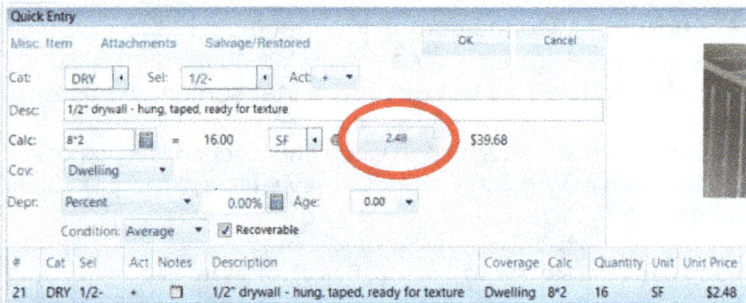

If you click on the "i" icon next to the price in this pop-out window, the detail window for "Item Activity Information" will pop up.

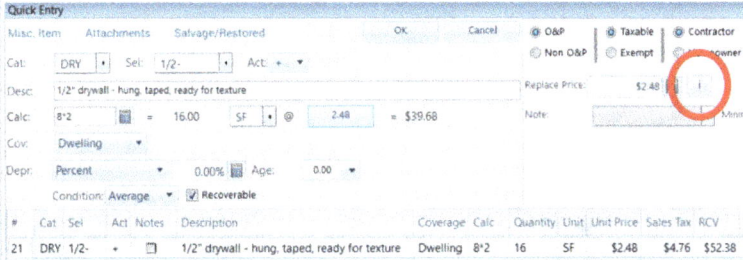

The Item Activity Information panel shows assumed costs for material, equipment, retail labor, market conditions, and the replacement price.

- Materials $0.62
- Equipment $0.00
- Retail Labor $1.86
- Market Conditions $0.00
- Replace Price $2.48

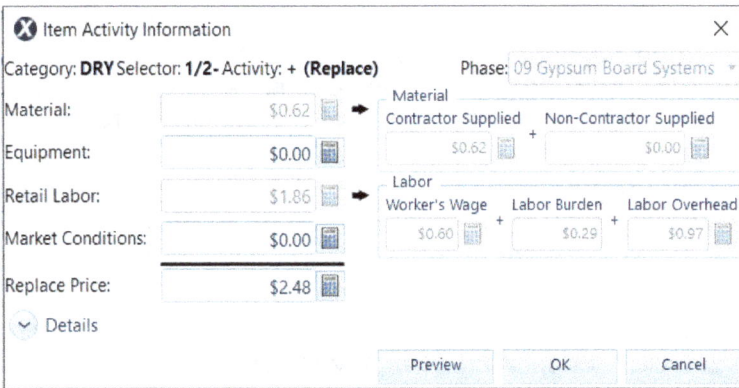

If you click on the downward arrow next to "Details" you will expose an additional menu.

Item Activity Information ✕

Category: **DRY** Selector: **1/2** - Activity: **+ (Replace)**   Phase: 09 Gypsum Board Systems

Material:	$0.62	
Equipment:	$0.00	
Retail Labor:	$1.86	
Market Conditions:	$0.00	
Replace Price:	$2.48	

Material
Contractor Supplied | Non-Contractor Supplied
$0.62 | + | $0.00

Labor
Worker's Wage | Labor Burden | Labor Overhead
$0.60 | + | $0.29 | + | $0.97

∧ Details

Type	Description	Price Per Unit	
Labor	Drywall Installer/Finisher	1.860	Add...
Material	Gypsum board, 1/2"	0.541	Edit...
Material	Metal corner bead	0.019	
Material	Drywall joint compound - 50 lb box	0.033	Delete
Material	Drywall nails (based on 25 to 50 lb box)	0.005	
Material	Drywall screws - grabber - (based on 25 to 50 lb box)	0.014	

Definition   Assembly Info   Supporting Events

Includes: Drywall, metal corner bead, joint compound (mud), drywall nails, joint tape, grabber screws, and installation labor.

Excludes:

Quality: 1/2" drywall, taped and floated, ready for a final texture (blown acoustic or stipple texture, etc.). This item is not intended to produce a surface that is ready for final paint.

Reference:

Green:

Notes: This item will include the following steps: tape coat, 1st coat, and 2nd coat sufficient to prep for an additional finish that needs to be applied such as heavy hand texture or sprayed acoustic.

Click for Detail

This expanded menu shows options for Definition, Assembly Info, and Supporting Events. The Definition details items such as Includes, Excludes, Quality, Reference, and Notes. For Labor - Drywall Installer/Finisher, the cost Includes in the Notes,

"This item will include the following steps: tape coat, 1st coat, and 2nd coat sufficient to prep for an additional finish that needs to be applied such as heavy hand texture or sprayed acoustic."

If you click "Supporting Events" you get a further breakdown of the assumptions built into the pricing including travel time.

Type	Description	Price Per Unit	
Labor	Drywall Installer/Finisher	1.860	Add...
Material	Gypsum board, 1/2"	0.541	Edit...
Material	Metal corner bead	0.019	
Material	Drywall joint compound - 50 lb box	0.033	Delete
Material	Drywall nails (based on 25 to 50 lb box)	0.005	
Material	Drywall screws - grabber - (based on 25 to 50 lb box)	0.014	

Definition   Assembly Info   Supporting Events

Labor assumption is based on an 8 hour day with 5 min planning, 60 min total drive time and mat/equ pick up, 20 min breaks, 40 min set-up/clean-up of tools and equipment, debris removal and floor sweeping or vacuuming in immediate workspace independent of any final cleaning at the end of the job if warranted, and 75 min overall loss of productivity from working in a restoration environment.

Preview   OK   Cancel

For example, "Supporting Events" for Drywall Installer/Finisher advise us,

"Labor assumption is based on an 8 hour day with 5 min planning, 60 min total drive time, and mat/equ pick up, 20 min breaks, 40 min set-up/clean-up of tools and equipment, debris removal and floor-sweeping or vacuuming in immediate workspace independent of any final cleaning at the end of the job if warranted, and 75 min overall loss of productivity from working in a restoration environment."

When was the last time you read a line item description or supporting events breakdown? Do you share these details with your project managers and production staff when they are planning their schedules or target completion dates?

In the Details breakout, select "Edit" to reveal the Labor Yield for this line item.

Details

Type	Description	Price Per Unit	
Labor	Drywall Installer/Finisher	1.860	Add...
Material	Gypsum board, 1/2"	0.541	Edit...
Material	Metal corner bead	0.019	
Material	Drywall joint compound - 50 lb box	0.033	Delete
Material	Drywall nails (based on 25 to 50 lb box)	0.005	
Material	Drywall screws - grabber - (based on 25 to 50 lb box)	0.014	

Definition | Assembly Info | Supporting Events

Type:	Labor	Direct Yield:	95.000
Component Code:		Component Price: $103.240/HR	
Supporting Events:	DRY-LAB	Yield:	55.416
	(41.667)	Price Per Unit:	$1.860
Description:	Drywall Installer/Finisher		
Yield = Direct Yield * (1 - (Supporting Events / 100))		Price Per Unit = Component Price / Yield	

Preview   OK   Cancel

You can edit the "Direct Yield" which will affect the "Yield" and "Price Per Unit".

<u>Default Yield:</u>
- Direct Yield = 95.00
- Component Price = $103.24/HR
- Yield = 55.416
- Price Per Unit = $1.86

The formulas, as stated, for Yield and Price Per Unit are:

- Yield = Direct Yield * (1 - (Supporting Events/100))
- = 95 x (1 - (41.667 / 100)
- = 95 x (1 - .41667)
- = 95 x .583
- Yield = 55.416

Price Per Unit = Component Price / Yield
- = $103.240 / 55.416
- = $1.860

In essence, if this were the only room we were repairing, the assumptions regarding productivity per laborer could be considered for revision. Rather than getting a full 8 hours of work from the technician, due to the smaller scope, we are losing productivity across the board in their ability to complete work at this site or anywhere else. If we had multiple rooms, perhaps the yield would be appropriate as they can move from room to room. With this sample alteration, the pricing reflects an attempt to recover some of this variance for labor.

I am not advocating for this as the best approach. Don't do this just because you saw it in this or any other book. Your estimating process should be exploring means and methods for the best use of whatever software you are incorporating into your business. Small jobs often suffer as they do not benefit from the economies of scale that are often assumed in unit pricing. The same can be true of production rate options.

In our Program Revised Estimate, we edited the Direct Yield from the default of 95 to 55. You can see this option in the top right of the "Assembly Info" breakout. This change brought our yield from 55.416 to 32.083 which raised our price per unit from $1.86 to $3.22.

Revised vs. Default Yield:
- Direct Yield = 55.00 (95.00)
- Component Price = Same $103.24/HR
- Yield = 32.083 (55.416)
- Price Per Unit = $3.22 ($1.86)

Supporting Events

Xactware Help for X1 states, "The Supporting events pane allows you to see calculations that modify the price such as waste or loss of productivity due to working in a restoration environment." Support events are indirect items necessary to complete the work at hand (direct repairs). Material waste due to handling and spillage factored at 5% would add 5 units for every 100.

As it relates to labor,

> *"The Supporting Events equate to the time which must be spent in addition to the labor that will be expended directly on the finished work product. Material pickup, tool and material setup (placement in the structure and readied for the job) and cleanup[42].*
> *"*

Direct Yield

Custom pricelist development and dissecting the inner workings of Xactimate are cornerstones in Ben Justesen's **Enlightened Restoration Solutions**[43] course. I appreciate that Ben is a contractor and his methods have been and are currently being tested in real world scenarios. Xactware continues,

> *"Direct Yield (that which applies exclusively to the finished product) is relatively easily determined while the calculation of Supporting Events for the structural repair industry is far more challenging. The pricing researcher must determine the average amount of time lost to Supporting Events. The Assumption is that this average amount will be sufficiently accurate for structural repair estimation."*

Xactware accounts for time and productivity losses, but you will want to confirm those calculations properly address the factors of your unique projects. Thankfully the software creators recognize there is a difference between a controlled

environment, such as those in the auto-repair industry, where the damaged product is brought to the repair vendor. On the other hand, restoration contractors never play with the comforts of the home. The Supporting Events are benchmarks for standardized pricing, they can, and in many cases, the assumptions should be adjusted.

---

[42] *Retail Labor Rates & Supporting Events*. Xactware.
http://xactware.custhelp.com/ci/fattach/get/77536/1355517791/redirect/1/filename/retail_labor_rates.pdf

[43] https://www.enlightenedrestorationsolutions.com/

"Because the structural repair industry works largely in an uncontrolled environment, situations occur where actual Supporting Events may dramatically differ from the assumed Supporting Events."

Even if you use something other than Xactimate, it is important to account for the nuances in your estimating process or you risk consistently short-scoping and therefore short-changing your production teams. For example, below is an old breakdown from Xactware outlining the updates to Xactimate 97, but the underlying principles are similar (if not the same).

Xactimate 97 Supporting Event Assumptions / Net Yield Calculation

Type	Component	Comp $	Direct	Spt Evnt %	Yield	$ Per Unit
LAB	CARP-FNC	34.60	2.000 EA/HR	47	1.060	32.642
MAT	DOR	78.353	1.000 EA/EA	00	1.000	78.353
MAT	FNCSHIMS	5.600	10.000 EA/BN	05	9.500	0.589
MAT	NAIL6F	1.013	1.095 EA/LB	05	1.038	0.976

Hard Costs: Lab: $32.64 Mat: $79.92 Equ: $0.00 = $112.56

Untaxed Unit Price: $112.56

Direct productivity shows here. The % of time or material lost to Supporting Events shows here and the Net Yield here.

The top line in the graphic reveals:
- Type as Labor (LAB)
- Component for Finish Carpentry (CARP-FNC) at $34.60
- Direct Yield at 2 Each/Hour
- Supporting Event at a factor of 47%
- Net Yield at 1.06
- Per Unit factor of $32.642

At the time of this update, Xactimate declared, "The bottom line is that by using Retail Labor Rates and Supporting Events, Xactimate 97 provides the structural repair industry an exciting opportunity for new levels of accuracy, openness, and fairness." That said, the information (transparency) is built into the program if you know where to look for it. Assumptions (or "Findings" as was the updated language for this version of Xactimate) are included in this breakdown:

- The Untaxed Unit Price of $112.56 includes $32.64 in labor and $79.92 in materials
- The finish carpenter can accomplish the "direct" installation of the door in 30 minutes or 2 doors per hour
- Direct Yield will be reduced by 47% when the Supporting Events are factored into the calculation
- Net Yield equals 1.06 doors per hour (at the Retail Labor Rate)

If you do not agree that your carpenter can install 1.06 doors per hour, you have to answer a few questions:

Are the rates and materials accurate? You would only know this if you dig into the assumptions of the program you are using (assuming they are as transparent as Xactimate).

Are the expectations realistic? If so, what can we do to train our carpenters to meet the goal? Especially items like minimizing trips to the hardware store for example.

Are the expectations unrealistic? If so, what can we do to communicate the real cost in our estimate? How do you advocate for yourself and the industry to elevate "standardized pricing" to reflect real-world costs?

In this chapter, we have reviewed these estimating examples and have dug deeper into estimating programs like Xactimate. Many of these resources are common to various estimating platforms and every organization will benefit from fine-tuning its skills. In the next chapter, we will explore three additional habits that contribute to better project outcomes.

Within your intentional estimating toolbag you now have:
- The Claims Standard
- A To-Scale Sketch and Numerous Labeled Photos
- A Simple Estimating Formula
- The Restoration Triangle
- Four Common Estimating Approaches

Module 5 Questions

1.   What are Supporting Events in Xactimate?

2.   What are indirect costs and how important are they to account for in your estimate?

3.   What does arbitrary means and how does it apply to the insurance claims process?

4.   How important is learning the ins-and-outs of your estimating program to achieving better project outcomes?

Additional Resources

Watch **this video** on *Common Estimating Shortfalls -* https://www.youtube.com/watch?v=sA-N9EkVCeE&t=1s

Read **this article** reviewing Bill Wilson's book *When Word's Collide -* https://insnerds.com/resolving-insurance-claims-disputes-with-bill-wilson-book-review-of-when-words-collide/

Watch **this video** on *Overhead and Profit for Insurance Claims - Markup vs. Margin -* https://www.youtube.com/watch?v=IRAqea55N5o

Read **this article** *Goldilocks the Adjuster & the Three Estimator Bears -* https://www.randrmagonline.com/articles/89129-goldilocks-the-adjuster-and-the-3-estimator-bears

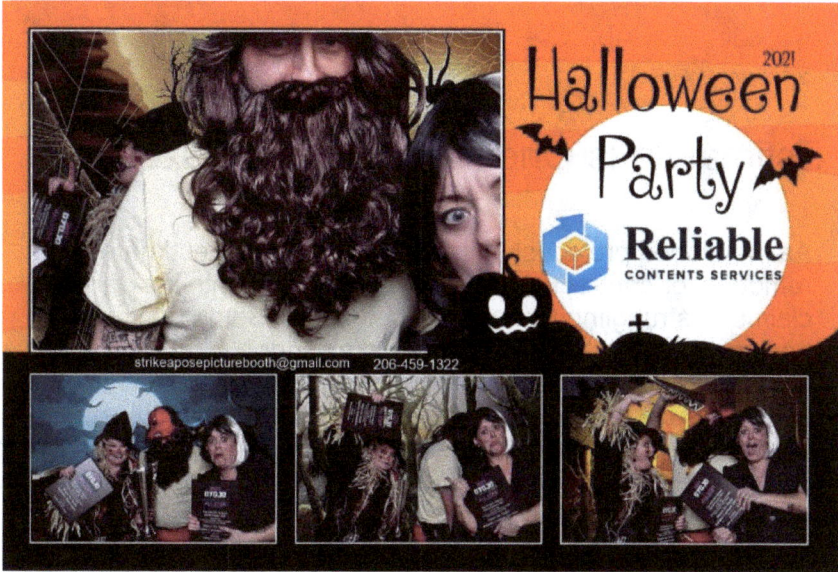

The author is pictured after officially losing The DYOJO Podcast SOCKTember 2021 by 4 pairs of socks to Sisters for Socks headed by Lindsey Ward (Reliable Contents Services) and Sarah Roberts (Superior Restoration). The picture was taken at the first annual Washington Restorers Costume Dance Party hosted by RCS.

Module Six

Estimating Is One Piece Of The Puzzle

As mentioned previously, I have written several estimates remotely for contractors who are transitioning into insurance claims or struggling with project outcomes. Some contractors have never used Xactimate and are exploring whether it is the right fit for them. Others have been using the program for estimating but underutilizing many of the other helpful aspects that can be derived from a well-written estimate. Good estimating software should provide helpful reports such as project budgets, work orders, material take-offs, etc.

Do you know what a **materials take-off** is? In a traditional construction estimating scenario, the materials take-off would be composed prior to the estimate. Why would this be important? First, whoever is doing the work of creating the estimate would be responsible to communicate the quantity and pricing of key materials factored into their agreed-upon scope. For some reason in property restoration, even for those that don't utilize Xactimate, this is not the norm.

When was the last time, prior to your costs hitting, you estimated the labor you thought would be involved to complete a project scope? When was the last time your organization provided your production team with cost details such as

quantities and budget for materials? How about the last time you calculated or tracked production rates for the primary scope items? Do you realize that if you use Xactimate, many of these factors are readily available?

Budgeting Approaches

For a simple broad view budget, we are going to take our prior Non-program Estimate which gave us **$332.68** and review some of the reporting options in Xactimate.

Grouping		
✚ Add	Filter (Off)	▾
Group	Subtotal	# Items
◢ 🖼 DRYWALL2		
🖼 Non Program	$332.68	7

You will remember this scope and cost includes the following line items from Xactimate:

#	Cat	Sel	Act	Notes	Description	Coverage	Calc	Quantity	Unit
14	DRY	1/2-	I	🗂	1/2" drywall - hung, taped, ready for texture -	Dwelling	8*2	16	SF
15	DRY	1/2-	M	🗂	1/2" drywall - hung, taped, ready for texture -	Dwelling	32	32	SF
16	DRY	PATCHJ	+	🗂	Tape joint for new to existing drywall - per LF	Dwelling	2+8+2	12	LF
18	PNT	S-	+	🗂¹	Seal the surface area w/PVA primer - one coat	Dwelling	10*3	30	SF
17	DRY	TEX	+	🗂	Texture drywall - light hand texture	Dwelling	10*3	30	SF
19	PNT	SP	+	🗂	Seal/prime then paint the surface area (2 coat	Dwelling	10*3	30	SF
20	PNT	P	+	🗂	Paint the surface area - one coat	Dwelling	12*8	96	SF

The Line Items Include:
- DRY ½- (install only) = ½" drywall - hung, taped, ready for texture at 8' long by 2' high (16SF)
- DRY ½- (material only) = ½" drywall - hung, taped, ready for texture at a full sheet (32SF) as this is the material minimum
- DRY PATCHJ = Tape joint for new to existing drywall - per LF at 2' up + 8' long + 2' down (12LF)
- DRY TEX = Texture drywall - light hand texture at 1' beyond the repair on all sides so 10' long by 3' high (30SF)
- PNT SP = Seal/prime then paint the surface area (2 coats) at the same 30SF as the texture application
- PNT P = Paint the surface area - one coat for the whole wall (corner to corner) 12' x 8' (96SF)

From the Reports tab in the Estimate Reports menu, we are going to select Final Draft and breakout the Recap by Category.

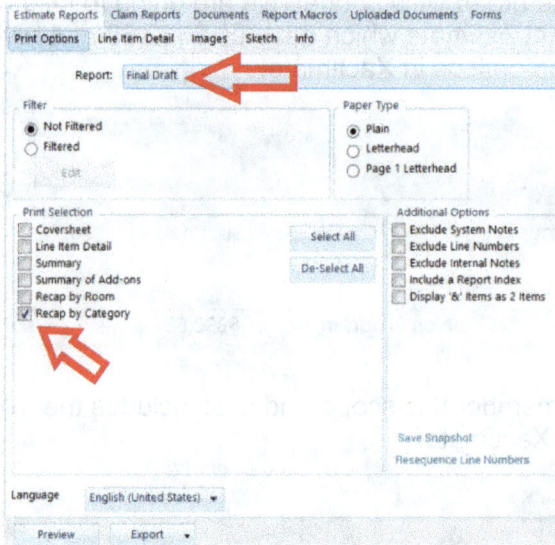

When we select "Preview" at the bottom of the page we will see the following Recap by Category details.

Recap by Category

O&P Items	Total	%
DRYWALL	490.47	48.58%
PAINTING	274.40	27.18%
O&P Items Subtotal	764.87	75.76%
Overhead	76.48	7.58%
Profit	76.48	7.58%
Sales Tax	91.79	9.09%
Total	1,009.62	100.00%

Simple Budget

Because I wrote all of the estimate examples in the same estimate, this shows the combined total for all five scenarios. For our project, we will create a simple (non-detailed) budget with a targeted profit margin of 30%. In this example, we have a simple scope to budget as the two primary categories are Drywall and Painting.

- $917.83 pre-tax sales price x .70 (to achieve 30% margin)
- = $642.48 materials and labor budget for drywall and paint with a 30% targeted margin
- *This is our budgeted cost of goods sold (COGs)

- $917.83 Sale (pre-tax)
- $642.48 COGs
- $275.35 Profit at 30% margin

By nature of the way Xactimate estimates are composed, with overhead and profit added to the end of an estimate as a **markup** (typically 20%), many contractors, consumers, and carrier representatives are confused about overhead and profit as a **margin**. Markup is a percentage of your costs. Margin is a percentage of your revenue (sale minus cost of goods sold).

An overhead markup is something added to an estimate, whereas an overhead margin is a figure that is calculated once actual costs are totaled. *All parties must understand the difference if the organization is going to achieve its overhead needs and its profitability goals.*

Ben Justesen and myself were tasked with presenting some simple definitions for clarifying the difference between markup

and margin. Prior to a full peer review, here were some of the elements we put forth:

Overhead and Profit

Definitions and distinctions in the difference between markup and margin. What you add (markup) versus what you make (margin).

Definitions:
- "Overhead & Profit" (O&P as a Markup %)
- General Overhead (as a Margin %)
- Net Profit (as a Margin %)

Markup

Revenue
- The income you earn by selling your products and services

Cost of Goods Sold (COGS)
- The costs (expenses) to create your products and provide your services

"Overhead & Profit" (O&P as a Markup %)
- AKA O&P added to the end of the estimate as a markup
- Overhead and Profit (O&P) is NOT the same as General Overhead and Net Profit
- Markup = Amount in which the cost of a product or service is increased in order to derive the sales price. This formula is a percentage of the cost.
- 10&10 (20%) markup actually results in a 16.67% margin (see infographic below)
- Contractors MUST understand that markup is NOT the same as margin

Markup Infographic

A 20% markup results in a 16.67% margin

$100.00	Estimated Costs
$20.00	**Markup** ($100 x 1.2)
$120.00	Sales price
$100.00	COGS
$20.00	Gross Profit
16.67%	Gross Profit **Margin** ($20 / $120)

Margin

Overhead Costs
- What it costs to run the business (indirect costs), and are separate from the COGS (direct costs)
- For example, Xactware states in their *Whitepaper on Overhead and Profit* that, "General Overhead are expenses incurred by a General Contractor, that cannot be attributed to individual projects, and include any and all

expenses necessary for the General Contractor to operate their business."

- Percentage of revenue (margin) as opposed to an "overhead and profit" markup which is a percentage of cost

Profit

- Sales Price - COGS (direct costs) = Gross Profit
- Gross Profit - General Overhead expenses (indirect costs) = Net Profit
- Net Profit is what you have after all COGS (direct costs) and general overhead (indirect costs) expenses have been accounted for
- Net Profit totals are the funds remaining to grow the business
- Xactware states, "Profit is typically added to the cost of a construction-related job to allow the entity performing the work to grow their company through reinvestment."
- General Overhead costs as an average + Net Profit goals = Budgeted Gross Margin
- If, for example, you calculate that your General Overhead goal is 30% and your Net Profit goal is 10% you would be seeking a 40% Budgeted Gross Margin
- Margin = Sales (Revenue) - The COGS. Percentage of revenue.

Margin Infographic

If your goal is a 40% margin

$100.00	Estimated Costs
$66.67	**Markup** ($100 / .60)
$166.67	Sales price
$100.00	COGS
$66.67	Gross Profit
40%	Gross Profit **Margin** ($66.67 / $166.67)

This book is primarily aimed at the internal functions of the estimating process. Before you can complain too loudly about external forces inflicting pain upon your company, you must do all in your power to identify and correct those self-inflicted habits that corrode your footing for growth. One nugget for those facing opposition to collecting overhead and profit on their projects comes from *Gilderman and Gilderman v. State Farm*, 649 A.2d 941 (Pa. Super. 1994) where a Pennsylvania court held that **the price of anything**—from a new roof to a new car—**includes profit for the craftsman or retailer**.

Breakout Budget

If we want to create a more detailed budget, we will need to know our estimated material costs so that we can separate these from our estimated labor costs. This is simple to find using the Components report in the same screen that we printed out Recap By Category from.

Again, select "Preview" from the bottom of the screen, and a report is generated.

Code	Description	Quantity	@	Unit Price	Total
DRY1/2	Gypsum board, 1/2"	37.85 SF	@	0.460	17.41
DRYCBEAD	Metal corner bead	1.78 LF	@	0.345	0.62*
DRYMUD	Drywall joint compound - 50 lb box	0.54 BX	@	11.979	6.50*
DRYN	Drywall nails (based on 25 to 50 lb box)	0.08 LB	@	1.766	0.15*
DRYSCREW	Drywall screws - grabber - (based on 25 to 50 lb box)	0.17 LB	@	2.730	0.46
DRYTAPE	Joint tape - 500' roll	0.05 RL	@	6.016	0.28*
PNTL	Latex paint	0.38 GL	@	41.942	16.10*
PNTPUT	Painter's putty	0.01 GL	@	21.067	0.29*
PNTSANDP	160 - 180 grit sandpaper - per sheet	0.21 SH	@	0.687	0.14
PNTSEALPVA	PVA - latex drywall primer/sealer	0.18 GL	@	19.240	3.45*
Total					**45.40**

The combined budget for materials for drywall and paint is $45.40. You can see this Components list is detailed, down to items such as corner bead, joint tape, painter's putty, and paint. This would also be what many contractors call a materials take-off. This report would be helpful to your subcontractors and carpenters as it provides them with what materials they will need to have with them to complete the job. If you want to reduce the amount of time your in-house labor spends at the hardware store, you can provide them with this list and tell them they should only shop once or you can have the materials delivered to the job.

Sample Budget Sheet

This is a sample budget made with a simple spreadsheet. These figures are designed to walk through a simplified process. If you have an existing process it likely is some variation of these basic metrics and principles.

Construction Job Budget

Job Name:	Non-Program Drywall		Job #					
Superintendent:								

Contract	Proposed Margin	Budget	Overhead	Material	Est Labor/Sub	Total Cost	Total cost w/ overhead	Under budget $ amount
$1,009.52	36%	$646.16	$50.48	$45.40	$549.48	$594.88	$645.36	$0.79
				2				

					LABOR & SUBS			
TRADE	orig line item $	sup or CO $	Budgeted total	PO Number	Labor/Sub Cost	Hours	Sub/in-house	
DRY	490.47		332.54	SH	330.00	13		
PNT	274.40		186.04	SH	166.00	7		
				SH		0		
Contingency				SH	50.48		Contingency of 5% if less than $5K , 2.5% if greater than $5K	
Base Service Charges								
TOTALS	$764.87	$0.00	$518.58		$549.48	20		

Budgeted Materials					Job Notes	
MATERIALS	Supplier	PO #	Cost			
Drywall & Paint	Lowes	SH	$45.40			
		SH				

All of the data entry points in this report are gathered from the Recap by Category

- Contract price
- Proposed (profit) margin
- Budget (contract price x proposed margin)
- Overhead in this case is direct or supervisory and is factored as a percentage of the contract price
- Material is totaled from the Budgeted Materials lower on the sheet
- Estimated Labor/Subcontractor is factored from the column totals in the section below
- The Under budget amount takes the Total cost with overhead from the Contract and reveals if there is a positive or negative variance

Details gathered from Recap by Category
- Labor and Subs
- You would build out your budget by carrying over each trade total from Recap by Category into the rows, for example:

DRY

- Original line item $ = $490.47 (comes directly from Recap)
- The budgeted total is the prior item-total x your factor for margin = $332.54 (budget)
- Labor/Sub Cost, in some cases you will round this number down or up, if you factor at $330.00 the Hours will factor at whatever amount you preset.
- Hours for our example labor is factored at $25/hr so $330.00 / $25/hr = 13 budgeted hours.

Details gathered from Components
Budgeted Materials

Assumptions
Proposed margin
Labor rate for hours extracted from labor/sub cost

				LABOR & SUBS			
TRADE	orig line item $	sup or CO $	Budgeted total	PO	Number	Labor/Sub Cost	Hours
DRY	490.47		332.54	SH		330.00	13
PNT	274.40		186.04	SH		169.00	7

Columns
- Trade = Categories from Recap by Category
- Orig Line Items = Line item budget from Recap by Category
- Budgeted Total = Line item $ x budget, for this exercise x 0.678
- Labor/Sub Cost = What you budget for the category minus the materials (if you choose)
- Hours = Labor/Sub Cost / average labor rate, for this exercise $25/hr

Breakdown (in-house labor)
- $45.40 Materials
- $330.00 Drywall labor, 13 hours at $25/hr
- $169.00 Paint labor, 7 hours at $25/hr
- $50.48 Overhead, 1.68 hours at $30/hr for supervisory
- $50.48 Contingency
- $645.36 Subtotal costs

If you are using in-house labor your work order might include the Scope and Components printouts from Xactimate with a budget of 22 hours for the carpenter in charge of the project.

				LABOR & SUBS			
TRADE	orig line item $	sup or CO $	Budgeted total	PO	Number	Labor/Sub Cost	Hours
DRY	490.47		332.54	SH		350.00	14
PNT	274.40		186.04	SH		195.00	8

Breakdown (subcontracted labor)
- $545.00 Drywall and paint, labor and materials
- $50.48 Overhead, 1.68 hours at $30/hr for supervisory
- $50.48 Contingency
- $645.96 Subtotal costs

Subcontractors vs. In-House Labor

I am of the opinion that when you subcontract the workout, you have more control over the cost but less control over the schedule. You may think you have your subcontractor nailed down, but that isn't always the case so you will want to build some buffers for job start and project duration.

Whereas with in-house labor, you have more control over the schedule but less control over the cost. If you have dedicated

labor, you have more direct control over the scheduling, but if you have shared in-house resources, scheduling can be as difficult as scheduling a subcontractor. This is a critical element of Chapter 8 in my book, *So, You Want To Be A Project Manager?*

Whatever tool you use for shared scheduling (aka The Board), it has to be the driver of your production planning. Each team member is responsible to plan and schedule their work in accordance with the availability of shared resources granted by **The Board**. Team members have to be accountable to each other by scheduling honestly. Dishonesty will cause the schedule and team trust to collapse.

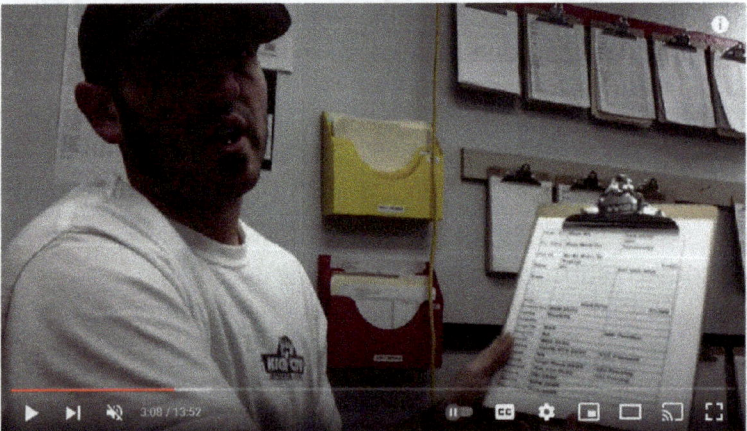

▶ ▶❙ 🔇 3:08 / 13:52   ⏸ CC ⚙ ▣ ▢ ⤴ ⛶

Create A Visible Schedule For Clear Communication

118 views • Apr 24, 2016   👍 1   👎 DISLIKE   ↪ SHARE   ≡+ SAVE   ...

This picture is a snip of a much younger me from my first

YouTube video. I am holding a clipboard for an individual project and you can see The Board, setup like a racetrack, for our work in progress (WIP). These points in the project lifecycle correspond with the DYOJO Project Tracker (see below).

What are the primary project lifecycle sequences?

- Customer information and contact
- Worksite inspection and scoping
- Estimate composition and transmission
- Claims negotiation and approval
- Contract and deposit
- Work start
- Change orders and supplements
- Punchlist (substantial completion)
- Final walk and Certificate of Complete (COC)
- Final billing and payment

Production Tracking

Why would we talk about project tracking or job management in a book about estimating? If you are asking that question, I would ask you to ask yourself a follow-up question, "Have you been listening at all?" **Estimating is not a silo**. Estimating is a key component within the chain of events that lead to a positive project outcome. This module will not be a deep dive into management structure or tracking resources but rather a skeletal overview of some of the factors that should be tracked within an organization.

A	B	C	D	K	L	M	O	P	Q	R	S	V	W	X
Who	Status	Last Name	First Name	Inspect	Scope	Est Sent	Rev	Appr	Contra	Deposi	Scope	Start	Punch	COC
		INSPECT / ESTIMATE												
		Johnson	John	1/2/21	1/2/21									
		ESTIMATE SENT												
		Johnson	Brad	1/2/21	1/2/21	1/3/21								
		APPROVED / CONTRACT												
		Johnson	Harold	1/2/21	1/2/21	1/3/21	1/6/21	1/8/21						
		PRODUCTION - WORK IN PROGRESS												
		Johnson	Max	1/2/21	1/2/21	1/3/21	1/6/21	1/8/21	1/9/21	1/9/21	1/10/21	1/15/21	2/2/21	2/7/21

The DYOJO Project Tracker is a simplified version of a customer management system using a free spreadsheet. You can create your own, use our simple template, or explore many of the well integrated systems available to restoration contractors. The driver behind this book is a course designed in collaboration with our friends at **Restoration Technical Institute** (RTI). I know their organization has teamed up with **iRestore** to build out and improve their restoration management system. Both entities have been (and hopefully will continue to be) sponsors of The DYOJO Podcast.

I believe systems created by restorers are the most likely to help restorers achieve their goals as the issues we face in our industry are unique within the skilled trades. Whatever you do, you must keep track of your projects as they progress through the key sequences in your production system. Ours is an entry level system, which, if used properly will help you create **clarity, consistency, and accountability** with your production team.

Developing and/or integrating this resource for your team is foundational to your success as it empowers your team members to be on the same page with regard to project status so that a revenue opportunity does not slip through the cracks.

If you are a solopreneur, you need to track key data points such as how referrals are coming in, where you are getting the most traction, what carrier you have the best conversion ratio with, etc. If you are an entrepreneur and you are building your team, collecting this data and reviewing it at least once a week with your team is critical to achieving your goals.

A	B	C	D	E	F	G	H	I
Who	Status	Last Name	First Name	Received	Intake	City	Carrier	Referral
		INSPECT / ESTIMATE						
		Johnson	John	1/1/21	EM	Tacoma	Allstate	ABC Restoration

What do you need to know about a project
- Name of the client
- When was the lead received
- Who was the first point of contact and complete the

Client Intake Form
- What city is the project in
- What carrier is the customer working with
- Who was the referral source

Why would these data collection points be important? <u>Can you answer the following process-related questions:</u>

When a customer contacts you, do you have a standardized process or intake sheet to ensure that you capture the details your team will need to respond?

Is there a shared file where the customer information is collected, updated, and accessible to all of your team members who will be involved in that project?

Can everyone see the current status of a job, who is responsible for the next steps, and have access to the customer notes leading up to them taking over the lead role on the project?

Questions two and three from above have more to do with developing a shared project file. For example, in Google, you can create a folder for all of your leads in the current year. A simple means of tracking when a lead was received includes using a naming convention for your files, one simple system is _ _ (last two numbers of the current year) _ _ (two-digit numbers of the current month). For example, if John Johnson calls in May of 2022, the folder name would be 2205 Johnson, John.

This folder would be accessible to everyone on the team who will be interacting with this customer and the first document in the folder would be the **Johnson, J Intake & Comms Notes**. Some teams prefer to use a separate document for New Client Intake and some combine those in the Comms Notes. If you are an owner or manager and want to discuss these resources, reach out to The DYOJO. Otherwise, I am assuming your organization uses some shared platform or software, and you will have to use that system.

Shared information that is accessible to all and updated in real-time is critical to your success. There are zero excuses for your team not to have this level of information at the ready and siloing job information will hurt your team. The elements of what I am sharing with regards to the DYOJO Project Tracker are foundational to integrating your processes. However you capture these details, they should be reviewed with your estimating and production staff at least once a week. The master categories include the following:

Inspect / Estimate
- When was a project received, and was it inspected within 72 hours (Common for Service Level Agreements or SLAs)?
- Where are we getting our leads from and how many do we need in order to keep our revenue wheel turning?

Estimate Sent

- When was the estimate sent, was it within 72 hours of the inspection?

Approved / Contract
- When was the estimate revised, approved, and translated into a contract?
- Are we converting leads into jobs?

Production - Work In Progress
- When was the deposit received and the file handed off to our production team?

Complete / Bill
- Are we hitting our cycle time goals? If we want happy customers and profitable jobs, our days in progress (DIP) is one of the key indicators of success - i.e. the longer a job is in progress the likelihood of negative impacts on customer satisfaction and profitability increases.

Closed Out Projects and customer reviews
- When a customer is not happy or does not understand what they owe, it impacts payment. We may not be able to convert every customer into a 5-star review, but are we consistently bringing repeat and referral business?

	Who	Status	Last Name	First Name	Received	Intake	City	Carrier	Referral	Called	Inspect	Scope	Est Sent
		INSPECT / ESTIMATE											
			Johnson	John	1/1/21	EM	Tacoma	Allstate	ABC Restoration	1/1/21	1/2/21	1/2/21	
		ESTIMATE SENT											
			Johnson	Brad	1/1/21	EM	Olympia	USAA	XYZ Water	1/1/21	1/2/21	1/2/21	1/3/21
		APPROVED / CONTRACT											
			Johnson	Harold	1/1/21	EM	Puyallup	State Far	123 Fire	1/1/21	1/2/21	1/2/21	1/3/21
		PRODUCTION - WORK IN PROGRESS											
			Johnson	Max	1/1/21	EM	Bremerton	Safeco	Google	1/1/21	1/2/21	1/2/21	1/3/21
		COMPLETE / BILL											
			Johnson	Carl	1/1/21	EM	Gig Harbo	AmFam	EM	1/1/21	1/2/21	1/2/21	1/3/21
		CLOSED OUT PROJECTS:											

As you can see, this process does not have to be complex, especially if you have a small to midsize operation. Before you can achieve **accountability**, you have to develop systems that are

clear and habits that are **consistent**. If you want to grow from working in your business, to working on your business, you need to develop processes that you can manage. If you are an estimator or an aspiring professional, you may not feel like you have much input into the overall structure of the organization. If you know what it should look like, you may be able to influence and contribute to your own unique process - you must develop CCA:

- Clarity
- Consistency
- Accountability

Build a system that is visible and hold people accountable to respect the process. Accountability starts with clear communication. If you want to build trust so that there will be teamwork, you must hold people responsible for their role in the process.

Clarity

Clarity is the foundation (mindset).

If a structure is compromised, we start to remove the finishes to expose the structural elements. Gaps in execution and failure to hit the mark on your goals trace themselves to the structure of the business as well. Clarity is the foundation that gets your team on the right mindset playing their role.

What real benchmarks (aka Key Performance Indicators, or KPIs) have you clarified to accompany the roles and responsibilities of your team members? As I said in the Preface, The DYOJO stands for The Do Your Own Job Dojo. In a young company the roles and responsibilities may be constantly evolving, but developing the structure to achieve your vision for success is important. People need to know, as clearly as possible, what they are responsible for and how they are doing in achieving those goals.

As Lisa Lavender shared, the first years of growth in her company were a blur. They had a vision for how they wanted to do business and they were intentional in tenaciously pursuing those goals. Lisa, like most business owners, realized there was a point when they needed to sit down to start formalizing the organization. As she shared, they recognized they didn't need to create the culture or the systems, they just needed to document, adapt, and improve them. They needed clarity so that they could scale with consistency.

Consistency

Consistency is the fuel (habit).

If team members have clarity on their responsibilities and consistency in executing their roles, the organization will have fuel to make progress on their goals. How often will you review everyone's performance? I recommend you meet with your team at least weekly and incorporate an open forum for discussing issues and resolutions together. Every role needs this collaborative and accountable interaction so they know what they can improve to help the team. Communicate that your team values helping each other work through issues, mistakes, and that failures are not fatal.

Gino Wickman, in his book *Traction*, outlines a three step process called **The Issues Solving Track** (aka IDS), which stands for:
- **I**dentifying the issue
- **D**iscussing the issue
- Working together to **S**olve the issue

If you really want to build accountability in your team, they need to have the forum and ability to call you out as well. If you are designing a structure and empowering a process, then everyone, including owners, managers, and estimators, must be accountable. Nothing will enhance teamwork more than the habit of candid discussions, (what my talented wife calls *having the [difficult] conversation*). Everyone should have the mindset that we can disagree but we are each working to build and improve our unique process together. Unfortunately, not everyone will see the value or being willing to be accountable. *Clarity is the soil and consistency is the fertilizer wherein accountability grows.*

Accountability

Accountability is the test.

Being intentional means we clarify our goals, develop consistency in our habits, and work together to raise the bar for ourselves and our team. If you want true accountability that will accelerate your growth, it must be top-down and bottom-up; everyone must be held to the same core standards.

To make progress in your goals, you need to bring your norms into sync with your expectations. People in a position of leadership need to download their what as well as their why for starting a business so that their team members can learn to execute the vision. Let's take a look at a few simple ways that you can help keep your team on track.

Norms & Expectations

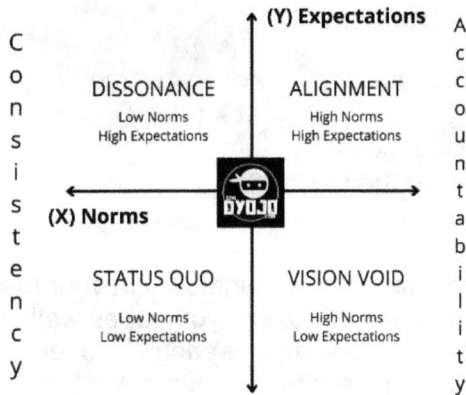

Norms are what you do. If you stand back and observe yourself and your team, what do you see? Are your actions in alignment with your stated vision, values, and objectives (or whatever words you use)? As we discuss several times in my second book, the question is not whether you have a culture, the question is whether you have been intentional in developing it. Do you communicate your expectations and do the norms you practice and/or allow follow those principles?

Clarity and consistency will lead to accountability. Alignment is the harmony between your expectations and your norms. You have to honestly assess, as a person in a position of leadership, what your outcomes are telling you about the efficacy of your efforts. Is your organization experiencing one of the following:

- (A) Dissonance
- (B) Status Quo
- (C) Vision Void
- (D) Alignment
- (E) Other

Expectations are both those that you declare as well as those that are understood. There often is dissonance between what is done and what is said. Expectations can also be revealed in how you hire, train, discipline, reward, promote, and fire. Similar to parenting, if you say one thing but do another or don't follow through, your team (like children) will continue to test just how far your boundaries can be pushed. An estimator or aspiring professional may serve as a team leader, so these principles would apply to those roles as well.

As a person in a position of leadership, you want to be intentional to develop the norms and expectations of your organization.

To the owner/manager

It is important to create a culture where team members can make honest mistakes and the group works together to source solutions. Mistakes are going to happen, you want to be in the know when they do so that you can propose a solution before the issue gets out of hand. The best way to ensure small problems don't become raging fires is for team members to understand that they should bring those items to you early and often. I introduced some thoughts on honest mistakes in my second book, *Be Intentional: Culture,* and expanded on *Mistakes, Mishaps, and Teaching Moments* in Chapter 11 of the book on project management.

To the estimator

While some have taken the stance that the contractor knows best so that means they shouldn't be questioned, this is unrealistic. If you know best, you should easily be able to explain what you are doing and why you are doing it. Our friend David Princeton, who specializes in claims advocacy, advises professionals to explain their why. The opposite can be effective as well, ask the carrier representative, "Can you please explain why you disagree with this scope item?" Whenever there are gaps in scope or cost, the estimator must share this information clearly with the production team.

The estimate drives the scope, cost, and duration of the project, and many of these items can be quickly accounted for when extracted from programs like Xactimate.

To the aspiring professional

Any opportunity for advancement starts with mastering your current roles and responsibilities. Be committed to learning to do whatever you are tasked with **the right way**, experiment with ways to be **efficient** (i.e. reduce inefficiencies), and elevate your ability to operate with **excellence**. Keep it simple, it starts with doing it right. Remember, in this industry, we get paid for what we document and as you move upward in a property restoration organization, the documentation is never less. Learn everything you can now and it will help you to progress by being of greater value to your company.

Within your intentional estimating toolbag you now have:
- The Claims Standard
- A To-Scale Sketch and Numerous Labeled Photos
- A Simple Estimating Formula
- The Restoration Triangle
- Four Common Estimating Approaches
- Some Tips for Budgeting, Tracking, & Accountability

Module 6 Questions

1. What report in Xactimate can you utilize for a simple (broad) budget?

2. What report in Xactimate can you utilize for materials takeoffs and budgeting?

3. If you want accountability what two elements do you need to start with cl_ _ _ _ _ and co_ _ _ _ _ _ _ _ _.

4. Why is project tracking important?

5. How important is it for every member of your team to have access to project files and information?

Additional Resources

For more information on budgeting read Chapter 7 from *So, You Want To Be A Project Manager?*

Read **this article** - *Skilled At Trades, Struggling With Business* - https://www.randrmagonline.com/articles/89097-skilled-at-trades-struggling-with-business

For more information on scheduling read Chapter 8 from *So, You Want To Be A Project Manager?*

Watch **this video** - *Create A Visible Schedule For Clear Communication* - https://www.youtube.com/watch?v=pP4kRZWCPG4&t=11s

For more on the *Norms and Expectations of a Strong Culture* read my **article** in *Claims Pages* - https://www.claimspages.com/editorials/2021/01/28/developing-the-norms-and-expectations-of-a-strong-culture/

Afterword

By Ed Cross, "The Restoration Lawyer,"
and Lily Atkins, "The Restoration Law Clerk"

In this book, Jon has done an admirable job of outlining a number of helpful estimating and communication strategies. He has become a unique asset to the restoration industry. Those who deliberately and methodically follow the steps will build successful businesses faster than their competitors.

But a great estimate does not pay the bills.

You have to collect on it.

Restoration collections are a vast, complex, and ever-changing process, but here, we outline some best practices we have observed restorers use successfully.

Communication failures cause many collection problems. Improving communication is key to increasing the bottom line. Communication is much more than speaking with others. There is also non-verbal communication, written, and visual. Think body language, contracts, change orders, text messages, emails, images, the appearance of the worksite, etc. The estimator performs the initial communication and data capture, which form the foundation for the contract.
Jon speaks to drafting a "defensible estimate." Assume that every invoice will be hotly contested and document your file accordingly. After a defensible estimate is created, the next important step is to create a rock-solid contract.

Restorers can improve communication by building a powerful restoration contract, documenting the file to be lucrative, staying in the loop for every adjuster communication, and developing and updating their own price lists.

There is an epidemic of vague contracts in the restoration industry. When files come into our law office, we often see documents simply titled "Work Authorization" with "TBD" as the price and two or three words about the scope. They are not contracts, and often create no legal duty to pay. Furthermore, with a vague contract or spaces left blank, the collection process may quickly decay into a "he said, she said" battle. The best practice is to fill in every space on the contract forms. The spaces are there for a reason! Ambiguous contracts may be construed against the restorer. The parties may be left at the court's mercy to decide what is fair rather than enforcing what the restorer believed the customer was agreeing to, or vice versa. One of the purposes of estimating is to give the stakeholders accurate information concerning the project scope and, therefore, the costs. **The estimate outlines the intended outcomes of a project and is intricately tied to a successful contract.**

A well-written contract lays out the understanding as to how each party will perform and how any disputes in the matter will be resolved. <u>A valid enforceable contract has five essential elements:</u> (1) identification of the parties; (2) thorough description of the scope and work; (3) price and payment terms; (4) time for completion; (5) notices and disclosures. The estimator plays a significant role in elements 2, 3, and 4, and an intentional estimator plays a role in all five.

As Jon notes "restoration contractors…should complete thorough data capture so that we can perform accurate data input." It is unfortunate the amount of documentation required of restorers to prove that they should be paid fair market value for work already performed. On the other hand, it is unavoidable. It may even increase profits and customer satisfaction. In our view, adjusters slash more money out of restoration invoices due to a lack of documentation than for any other reason. **Some restorers have the documentation but have not taken the time to organize it or present it in a usable form.**

Imagine yourself in the carrier's shoes:

>   *If you can't show us what you did, we don't know you did it;*

If you can't show us why you did it, we won't know if it was necessary;

If you can't show us who did it, it will be difficult to investigate.

To collect a fair price, you may need to show that you would prevail if you went to court to collect. To prevail on a claim for breach of contract, the contractor has the burden of proving, among other things, the existence of a valid and binding contract, a commitment to pay, the performance of the work, and non-payment by the customer. So the file needs to tell that story. A person uninvolved in the project should be able to open the file and understand what occurred, where, when, and why. **The documentation should reveal compelling reasons why you should be paid what you charged and how the work was performed carefully.**

Policyholders often receive conflicting messages from restorers and adjusters. This puts the policyholder in a precarious position, wondering whom to trust. Be sure that you do everything in your power to form a relationship of trust with the customer. Vigorously train project managers on the meaning and significance of the terms of the contract and require them to explain the terms to customers before they sign. They should also explain to the customer how claims adjusting works and explain that some insurance companies look for ways to cut corners to save themselves money. Explain The Claim Standard: *To restore the property to resemble pre-loss conditions, with materials of like kind and quality (LKQ); no more and no less.*

Unfortunately, some adjusters are overzealous and push for results that will not make the policyholder whole. Sadly, some of them try to turn the policyholder against the restorer. This wreaks havoc on a restoration business. However, the policyholder's goal to be made whole is perfectly aligned with the restorer's goal to perform the work properly, using LKQ materials. This unity of interest presents a wonderful opportunity for the restorer to form an alliance with the policyholder. **The restorer should try to persuade the policyholder to insist on the restorer's presence for every communication with the adjuster related to the project.** We strongly agree with the advice of pricing guru Ben Justesen of Enlightened Restoration Solutions who recommends that restorers "cc:" the customer on all email correspondence with the adjuster. If the adjuster responds without including the customer, bring the customer back into the loop by cc'ing the customer again.

If you are present for every significant communication with the adjuster, you can increase the chance you will be allowed to do the job correctly. In most states, it is a crime to provide policy interpretations or represent a policyholder in a claim without an adjuster's license. However, you are entitled to represent yourself and talk about the price and scope for your benefit. Do not hold yourself out as a representative of the policyholder.

Creating your own price list will help you earn a fair price for your work, and it helps the industry in the long term. Every project is unique, every customer is unique, and there is a unique level of service provided to each customer. Adjusters cannot prohibit deviation from standardized price lists without the consent of the restoration contractor, e.g., through a TPA agreement. Every time an adjuster tells you, "there's a contractor across town who will do it for less," you should push back hard. Explain that carriers owe the usual and customary cost of the work as established in the competitive marketplace––not the lowest price in town, and not necessarily the Xactimate price. No policy limits the carrier's liability to the prices stated in Xactimate. Carriers that don't fulfill obligations under a policy may be liable for breach of the insurance contract and insurance bad faith. Properly-drafted assignments of insurance rights put contractors in a first-party position under the policy. In most states, this allows the contractor to pursue breach of contract and bad faith claims directly against the carrier.

Make your own prices based on the needs of your company and the values in your market. Provide regular and frequent price feedback to the publishers of your estimating software. Ben Justesen teaches an excellent course that helps

restoration contractors master the science of customizing their prices. He covers the pricing methodology, what has worked and not worked, how to determine labor rates, create a price list, and how to provide pricing feedback. Feedback helps the publishers of standardized price lists to update their prices.

The contractor is responsible for the scope of repairs as outlined in the contract. The insurer is held to the duty outlined in the insurance contract, the laws interpreting the contract, and insurance regulations. The carriers must err on the side of coverage and always engage in fair claims handling practices. Adjusters cannot invent their own exclusions or limitations.

Common tactics such as price slashing may win you a project today but may not be the best means to ensure that you are profitable for the long term. The promises we provide our customers to secure the project should be consistent with how we execute and complete the job.

In the end, a happy customer and a paid invoice is the ultimate goal. Good documentation and communication solve many common collection challenges. The key takeaways are: build a strong bond with the policyholder based on a relationship of trust, stay in the loop for all substantive communications, and create documentation that speaks for itself. Do high-quality work for a fair price. Send the invoice to the customer with a courtesy copy to the adjuster, and then be persistent but polite!

Good luck.

More from The DYOJO

Book 1 - thedyojo.com/book1
Be Intentional: Estimating
"You Suck At Estimating" was a title Isaacson initially considered. Jeff Moore, President of ATI talked Isaacson out of going with this title and he was probably right to do so, but a part of me wishes Isaacson moved forward with his original title. Why? Because a lot of you suck at estimating. There I said it, and Isaacson does a masterful job to imply this reality at the outset of Be Intentional: Estimating." **- Whatley**

Book 2 – thedyojo.com/book2
Be Intentional: Culture
"This book provides so many different insights that the reader can understand where everyone in a team is coming from, not just from people in a position of management. The information and experience from all walks of life paints a clear picture on how people can approach leadership." **- David Smith**

Book 3 – thedyojo.com/book3
So, You Want To Be A Project Manager?
"This book covers all the good, the bad, and the ugly of being a Project Manager. The information was so well laid out and processed that I keep extra copies in my office now to hand out to those that I know will benefit from it." **- Gordy Powell**

The DYOJO Podcast – thedyojo.com/podcast
Thursdays are for **The DYOJO Podcast** - *INFOtainment to help you shorten your DANG learning curve.* Listen on Apple, Spotify, and Google Podcasts or watch on YouTube. New episodes release on Thursdays.

PropertyRestorationHistory.com
This is a labor of love. We are working to track down and piece together elements of the history and rise of the property restoration industry. This effort will include aspects of carpet cleaners becoming water damage mitigation specialists, the evolution of fire damage restoration, integration of insurance claims repairs, and the emergence of what we now call property restoration professionals.

Additional Thanks Yous

Thank you to co-editor Tiffany Acuff for her patience in working alongside The DYOJO. Even though she is now working for the "other" side, she has a passion for learning and elevating the property restoration industry which fuels her efforts to help me edit my ramblings.

Thank you to those who took time out of their busy schedules to peer-review portions of this book and provide incredibly helpful and honest feedback (including the testimonials at the opening) which contributed to improving the content you have just consumed.

www.ingramcontent.com/pod-product-compliance
Lightning Source LLC
Chambersburg PA
CBHW072156270326
41930CB00011B/2447